CLAIMING DISABILITY

CLAIMING DISABILITY

KNOWLEDGE AND IDENTITY

SIMI LINTON

FOREWARD BY MICHAEL BÉRUBÉ

NEW YORK UNIVERSITY PRESS
NEW YORK AND LONDON

NEW YORK UNIVERSITY PRESS
New York and London

Library of Congress Cataloging-in-Publication Data
Linton, Simi, 1947–
Claiming disability : knowledge and identity / Simi Linton.
p.   cm. — (Cultural front (Series))
Includes bibliographical references and index.
ISBN 0-8147-5133-4 (cloth : acid-free paper). — ISBN
0-8147-5134-2 (paper : acid-free paper)
1. Disability studies.   2. Sociology of disability.   I. Title.
II. Series.
HV1568.2.L55   1998
305.9'0816 — dc21   97-21218
                                                          CIP

New York University Press books are printed on acid-free paper,
and their binding materials are chosen for strength and durability.

Manufactured in the United States of America

10 9 8 7 6 5

CONTENTS

FOREWORD

PRESSING THE CLAIM

In the years and decades to come, inside academe and outside, "claiming disability" is sure to become one of the most politically sensitive endeavors a body can undertake. That's partly because the U.S. population will be gradually aging, and with age comes a certain vulnerability to the fleshy frailties of body and mind; but it's also because *disability* will have so multifarious and indeterminate a meaning in U.S. culture, regardless of how old our average citizen may be. For "disability" is the most labile and pliable of categories: it names thousands of human conditions and varieties of impairment, from the slight to the severe, from imperceptible physical incapacity to inexplicable developmental delay. It is a category whose constituency is contingency itself. Any of us who identify as "nondisabled" must know that our self-designation is inevitably temporary, and that a car crash, a virus, a degenerative genetic disease, or a precedent-setting legal decision could change our status in ways over which we have no control whatsoever. If it is obvious why most nondisabled people resist this line of thinking, it should be equally obvious why that resistance must somehow be overcome.

Thus the definition of *disability*, like the definition of *illness*, is inevitably a matter of social debate and social construction: as Simi Linton shows time and again in these pages, humans have defined *normal* in as many ways as there are human cultures. In the wake of the Americans with Disabilities Act of 1990, "claiming disability" will involve taking up a contested place in an intricate sociolegal apparatus, and consequently, few social imperatives will be as pressing as our need to enrich and enhance our culture's collective understanding of disability—in its causes, its effects, its representations, and its ramifications. What Linton shows us in *Claiming Disability*, crucially, is that universities will not be able to meet that pressing need if "disability" remains a subject confined to the "applied fields" such as social work or rehabilitation; in other words, if disability is not understood in terms of its complex, overdetermined and sometimes tenuous relations to identity, it will not be sufficiently incorporated into the curriculum of the liberal arts or into the definition of what constitutes "the humanities." And if we do not imagine "disability" as a broad, general subject that shapes the humanities, it is all the less likely that we will manage to imagine disability as a broad, general subject that shapes public life and public policy.

But I should back up for a moment and confess that I did not always think this way. (Indeed, I hope my own change of mind will serve as evidence of the cogency of Linton's argument.) Once upon a time, I did not see what "disability studies" might have to do with me. I had what I thought was a liberal, open-minded attitude toward mental and physical disabilities; I was kind to people who used wheelchairs (and mindful of whether they did or didn't welcome my physical assistance with doors) and respectful of all persons regardless of their mental abilities, but when it came to whether disability should be a major academic subject, I just couldn't see the point of one more "additive" studies program in the curriculum. In the early 1990s, for instance, I read newspaper reports of a controversy at Hunter College over the status of disability studies. Apparently there had been some dispute over whether "disability" should be included in the subjects approved for general education courses; the advocates of disability studies had lost the battle, and their protests were depicted, in the argot of that bygone era, as one more instance of the tide of "political correctness" sweeping through the groves of academe. Of course, even then I knew better than to believe what I read in the papers. But though I was properly outraged at the way the New Right was trying to scandalize women's studies, African American studies, and area studies of all kinds, I honestly didn't think that disability studies merited the same kinds of claims—or the same kind of defense.

As best I can recall at this distance, my reasoning depended on a calculation of centers and margins—a calculation that I somehow exempted from the deconstruction I had been trained to apply to all such calculations. The calculation ran something like this: "general education" should involve broad introductory courses in history, literature, science, philosophy, and political theory. Perhaps after those course requirements are fulfilled, students can choose elective courses in "specializations" like disability studies, but disability studies is by definition *not general;* it is specific only to disability. Look at the field of education, for instance: general education is general, and "special" education is . . . well . . . *special,* is it not?

As it turns out, of course, Simi Linton herself was a central player in the controversy at Hunter; this book is (in part) a result of that curricular dispute over the centrality of disability studies. And, more importantly, Simi Linton was *right*, and together with a handful of scholars in this small but growing field, she has convinced me that disability studies is no more an optional "additive" to the liberal arts than is the study of gender or race. Part of the reason I changed my mind so dramatically has nothing to do with anything I've read; when I became the father of a child with Down syndrome, I realized immediately and viscerally that disability can happen to anyone—including someone very close to you, and including you, too. But experience is not my only teacher: reading scholars like Rosemarie Garland Thomson and Lennard Davis, essayists like Nancy Mairs and Leah Hager Cohen, I began to encounter and understand various constituencies within the disability community from Down syndrome associations to deaf culture.

Today, when I try to account for my relation to disability studies as a nondisabled scholar, I am not merely appalled but intrigued by my former conviction that disability studies is not sufficiently "central" to the liberal arts. I now believe that my resistance to disability studies is of a piece with a larger and more insidious cultural form of resistance whereby nondisabled people find it difficult or undesirable to imagine that disability law is central to civil rights legislation. Here's what I mean. Just as I was "liberal" with regard to disability, so was I "liberal" with regard to gender and race: I supported (and I continue to support) equal pay for equal work and initiatives such as affirmative action *regardless of whether those initiatives would ever benefit me*. I did not fear that I would become black or Hispanic someday; I was not reserving the right to a sex-change operation; I simply supported civil rights with regard to race and gender because I regarded these as long overdue attempts to make good on the promise of universal human rights. It is for the same reason that I support gay and lesbian rights today, with regard to marriage, housing, childrearing, and employment. But for some reason, *even though disability law might someday pertain to me*,

I could not imagine it as central to the project of establishing egalitarian civil rights in a social democracy. Gender, race, sexual orientation—these seemed to me to be potentially universal categories even if I myself wound up on the privileged side of each; disability, by contrast, seemed too specific, too . . . *special* a category of human experience.

The irony, of course, is precisely this: even though I knew that gender, race, and sexual orientation were unstable designations, subject to all manner of social and historical vicissitudes, I had yet to learn—or to be taught—that disability is perhaps the most unstable designation of them all. Surely I was in denial, as are so many nondisabled persons; but then, there's an odd thing about being in denial, you know. When you're told you're in denial, you tend to deny it.

Thanks to scholars like Simi Linton, however, I've come to believe that the study of disability has its place in the curriculum—and that place is everywhere. Whether we're studying the history of public policy with regard to mental illness, or the social status of epileptics in non-Western cultures, or the depiction of disability in the novels of Toni Morrison, or the ramifications of developmental delays for theories of social justice, or models of language acquisition, or, indeed, the very construction of intelligence itself—the understanding of disability can—*and should be*—central to what we do in universities. More specifically, as Simi Linton shows us, it should be central to what we do in the humanities. And perhaps, just perhaps, if disability is understood as central to the humanities, it will eventually be understood as central to *humanity*—in theory and in practice, in sickness and in health, in cultural studies as in public policy. Few claims on our attention, I think, could be more pressing.

Michael Bérubé
University of Illinois
Urbana-Champaign

ACKNOWLEDGMENTS

My thoughts here begin and end with David.

In between, those thoughts turn to my family and friends, North, East, South, and West. They are my bookends.

My thoughts linger on all of the disabled women and men, and allies, who form my community, and rest on a number who have been invaluable in shaping this book: Barbara Waxman-Fiduccia, Corbett O'Toole, Marsha Saxton, Paul Longmore, Anthony Tussler, Adrienne Asch, Harlan Hahn, Steve Brown, David Pfeiffer, Kate Seelman, the late Irv Zola, and others, mentioned below. I can't imagine a more astute, and irreverent group of friends and colleagues, a more enveloping community, a stronger more committed group of activists and scholars.

Significantly, Harilyn Rousso and Rosemarie Garland Thomson were irreplaceable. They read gallons of words and thought through every large and small problem with me. And made it fun and delicious.

Conversations with the MLA dinner committee (Lennard Davis, Brenda Brueggeman, Georgina Kleege, Ellen Steckert, David Mitchell, Sharon Snyder, Nancy Mairs, Phyllis Franklin, Harilyn Rousso, and Rosemarie Garland Thomson) and with the members of the Society for Disability Studies bedroom committees convinced me that disability studies was the most invigorating home base from which to work.

Many people read or heard pieces of the manuscript and were generous with their time and incisive in their thinking. Thank you all: Lee Bell, Tanis Doe, Carol Gill, Rickie Solinger, Elizabeth Kamarck Minnich, Phyllis Rubenfeld, Stanley Aronowitz, Michelle Fine, Sonia Nieto, Paula Mayhew, Richard Weiner, Mike Hill, Dorothy Helly, Michael Bérubé, and Bob Vorlicky.

It was with my colleagues Susan Mello and John O'Neill at the Disability Studies Project at Hunter that I first began to formulate the ideas for this book. They contributed ideas, words, roast beef sandwiches, and loads of inspiration.

Thanks to my assistants, particularly Myrtilda Tomlinson, Michelle Malek, Zachery Miller, and Julie Smore, for all their help.

Great thanks to Eric Zinner, my editor at New York University Press, and to Michael Bérubé, the editor of the Cultural Front series that I am privileged to be a part of.

The National Institute of Disability and Rehabilitation Research provided the Switzer Distinguished Fellowship that gave me the time to conduct the research and to write. Thank you for that support.

Great thanks to my sister, Florence Weiner, for forging a path as the first writer in the family, for her commitments, her moral center, and for her wonderful, wacky take on the world.

And I acknowledge, with great gusto and love, David, the gravity and helium in my life, the smartest man on eight wheels, the delight of all time.

RECLAMATION

The curriculum is a manifest expression of the cultural values just as laws are manifest expressions of what a society deems to be right or wrong behavior.   Kliebard 1992, 199

Our educational institutions . . . are, not alone but preeminently, the shapers and guardians of cultural memory and hence of cultural meanings.   Minnich 1990, 12

It was, at one time, seamless. There were no disjunctures between the dominant cultural narrative of disability and the academic narrative. They supported and defended each other. But in the past twenty years, as the flaws in the civic response to disability have been exposed, as changing social structures and legislative victories reassemble that narrative, the academic tale slips further behind. It neither reflects the change that has occurred nor offers the space or the means to think in more progressive ways about disability.

Enter disability studies: a location and a means to think critically about disability, a juncture that can serve both academic discourse and social change. Disability studies provides the means to hold academics accountable for the veracity and the social consequences of their work, just as activism has served to hold the community, the education system, and the legislature accountable for disabled people's compromised social position.

This book examines disability studies as a field of inquiry, its historical roots, present configuration, and explanatory value. Disability studies takes for its subject matter not simply the variations that exist in human behavior, appearance, functioning, sensory acuity, and cognitive processing but, more crucially, the meaning we make of those variations. The field explores the critical divisions our society makes in creating the normal versus the pathological, the insider versus the outsider, or the competent citizen versus the ward of the state. It is an interdisciplinary field based on a sociopolitical analysis of disability and informed both by the knowledge base and methodologies used in the traditional liberal arts, and by conceptualizations and approaches developed in areas of the new scholarship. Disability studies has emerged as a logical base for examination of the construction and function of "disability." These scholarly explorations and the initiatives undertaken by the disability rights movement have resulted in new paradigms used to understand disability as a social, political, and cultural phenomenon.

Disability studies has arisen in the past twenty years to focus an organized critique on the constricted, inadequate, and inaccurate conceptualizations of disability that have dominated academic inquiry. Above all, the critique includes a challenge to the notion that disability is primarily a medical category. Consequently, disability studies contests the current academic division of labor in which the study of the phenomenon rests in the specialized applied fields (rehabilitation, special education, health, and so on) and the rest of the academy is largely exempt from meaningful inquiry into the subject of disability. By refusing the medicalization of disability and by reframing disability as a designation having primarily social and political significance, disability studies points to the inadequacy of the entire curriculum with respect to the study of disability. The fault lines that have been exposed stretch from one end of the curriculum to the other: from cultural studies to American studies, from women's studies to African American studies, from biology to literary criticism, from history to psychology, and from special education to philosophy.

Despite the steady growth of scholarship and courses, particularly in the past five years, the field of disability studies is even more marginal in the academic culture than disabled people are in the civic culture. The enormous energy society expends keeping people with disabilities sequestered and in subordinate positions is matched by the academy's effort to justify that isolation and oppression.

Disabled people, and I will immediately identify myself as one, are a group only recently entering everyday civic life. A host of factors have typically screened us from public view. We have been hidden—whether in the institutions that have confined us, the attics and basements that sheltered our family's shame, the "special" schools and classrooms designed to solve the problems we are thought to represent, or riding in segregated transportation, those "invalid" coaches, that shuttle disabled people from one of these venues to another. The public has gotten so used to these screens that as we are now emerging, upping the ante on the demands for a truly inclusive society, we disrupt the social order. We further confound expectations when we have the temerity to emerge as forthright and resourceful people, nothing like the self-loathing, docile, bitter, or insentient fictional versions of ourselves the public is more used to.

We have come out not with brown woollen lap robes over our withered legs or dark glasses over our pale eyes but in shorts and sandals, in overalls and business suits, dressed for play and work—straightforward, unmasked, and unapologetic.[1] We are, as Crosby, Stills, and Nash told their Woodstock audience, letting our "freak flag fly." And we are not only the high-toned wheelchair athletes seen in recent television ads but the gangly, pudgy, lumpy, and bumpy of us, declaring that shame will no longer structure our wardrobe or our discourse. We are everywhere these days, wheeling and loping down the street, tapping our canes, sucking on our breathing tubes, following our guide dogs, puffing and sipping on the mouth sticks that propel our motorized chairs. We may drool, hear voices, speak in staccato syllables, wear catheters to collect our urine, or live with a compromised immune system. We are all bound together, not by this list of our collective symptoms but by the social and political circumstances that have forged us as a group. We have found one another and found a voice to express not despair at our fate but outrage at our social positioning. Our symptoms, though sometimes painful, scary, unpleasant, or difficult to manage, are nevertheless part of the dailiness of life. They exist and have existed in all communities throughout time. What we rail against are the strategies used to deprive us of rights, opportunity, and the pursuit of pleasure.

It is our closeted selves that have been naturalized within the academic curriculum. Even a cursory review of the curriculum reveals only patronizing and distorted representations of disability, and these are left largely unexamined and unchallenged. But minor housecleaning will not rid out the deeper structural elements, the scholarly conventions, and theoretical underpinnings within which those representations are deemed valid and useful. A closer look reveals problems in both the structure and content of the curriculum, predicated on a narrowly conceived interpretation of disability.

The field of disability studies is now at a critical juncture; scholars and activists have demonstrated that disability is socially constructed to serve certain ends, but now it behooves us to demonstrate how knowledge about disability is socially produced to uphold existing practices. I attempt to capture this critical moment here in a stop-action photo that reveals that terrain. Yet this is also a strategic endeavor not only to mark the moment and the territory but also to stake out the contested borders where the resistance to the ideas is strongest.

Having appointed myself as navigator, I should comment on my identity as a disabled woman. The particulars of my condition are not of concern. They may impinge on specific pieces of the puzzle I am trying to assemble here, and I will discuss them in that context, but they are of little consequence to this overview. Disabled people, across the broadest spectrum of disability, have solidified as a group. Although this group identity has certainly not been comfortably embraced by all disabled people, a strong disability alliance has led to civil rights victories and the foundation of a clearly identified disabled community. The cultural narrative[2] of this community incorporates a fair share of adversity and struggle, but it is also, and significantly, an account of a world negotiated *from the vantage point of the atypical.* Although the dominant culture describes that atypical experience as deficit and loss, the disabled community's narrative recounts it in more complex ways. The cultural stuff of the community is the creative response to atypical experience, the adaptive maneuvers through a world configured for nondisabled people. The material that binds us is the art of finding one another, of identifying and naming disability in a world reluctant to discuss it, and of unearthing historically and culturally significant material that relates to our experience.

In the absence of the specifics of my condition, and my life, you may find yourself conjuring up some of the readily available images of disabled women, both fictional and real: the beholden Blind Girl in Chaplin's *City Lights;* the shame-riven Laura Wingfield in *The Glass Menagerie;* the doleful poster child gazing up at you from the collection box on the supermarket checkout counter; the defiant disability rights activist arrested for civil disobedience; your neighbor down the hall—or you may see yourself. We all share a cultural space. I don't claim to speak to every person's experience, only to paint myself within this frame. My experience as a disabled subject and my alliance with the community are a source of identity, motivation, and information.

I am also, by discipline, a psychologist, but this essay is informed more directly by women's studies, queer studies, cultural studies, the field of disciplinarity, and, of course, disability studies than by my training. In fact, some basic tenets of psychology run counter to core ideas in disability studies in at least three fundamental ways. First, psychology is responsible for the formulations and research conventions that cement the ideas of "normal," "deviant," "abnormal," and "pathology" in place. The fact that disability is inextricably linked to pathology is problematic, but even more fundamental is psychology's endorsement of the idea of "normalcy," which centers and privileges certain types of behavior, functioning, and appearance. Second, psychology's emphasis on empiricism and its repudiation of standpoint theory or positionality as legitimate starting points for research work against the types of qualitative, interpretive, historical analyses necessary to explicate the social construction of disability, the meanings assigned to disability, and the policies and practices that oppress disabled people. Oliver discusses this issue in a somewhat different way when he notes that the "social relations of research production . . . are built upon a firm distinction between the researcher and the researched" (Oliver 1992, 102). Third, although there are exceptions, psychology primarily trains practitioners to intervene on the personal level rather than intervene to alter the environment. Psychology in general has traditionally focused attention on "the personal qualities of those defined as having or being the problem," and, as a result, the policy derived from that research addresses "person-fixing rather than context-changing" (Trickett, Watts, and Birman 1994, 18). Disability studies, in contrast, focuses on the external variables: the social, political, and intellectual contingencies that shape meaning and behavior.

The questions that psychology and other traditional disciplines ask, and the methods and practices found in those disciplines are insufficient for addressing the problems that disability studies sets out to solve. These limitations aside, I must add that I have found my clinical training useful not in fostering disability studies but in analyzing the strength of the resistance I've witnessed over the years to disability studies and to disabled people's perspective.

I hope in this book on disability to bring into stark relief, to foreground, the mechanisms by which disability is covered over, layered with meaning and rendered invisible. This book is an effort to turn those processes inside out and reveal them to be not inevitable reactions to human conditions labeled disabilities but devices used to sort human beings according to the social and economic needs of a society. The disability rights movement has paved the way for an investigation of this sort. By calling attention to the patterns of discrimination, by creating unity across previously divided constituencies, and by forging a potent and effective civil rights and social justice movement, it has challenged the academic community to reckon with its own role in this process. The scholarship and curriculum practices housed in academic institutions play a significant role in the perpetuation of a divided and unequal society. The academy has only just begun to examine how its paltry and lopsided vision of disability compromises the knowledge base. Therefore, this book examines the consequences of these constricted views on disabled people's lives and on the knowledge that we impart to students. It uses as its main text the academic culture that constructs that knowledge and participates in the construction of those lives.

NOTES

1. The unapologetic stance is given its full recognition in the aptly named book *No Apologies: Making It with a Disability* (Weiner 1986).
2. For further information on ideas on disability as culture see Steve Brown's monograph *Investigating a Culture of Disability* (1994). It is available from the Institute on Disability Culture, 2260 Sunrise Point Road, Las Cruces, New Mexico 88011.

2

REASSIGNING MEANING

The present examination of disability has no need for the medical language of symptoms and diagnostic categories. Disability studies looks to different kinds of signifiers and the identification of different kinds of syndromes for its material. The elements of interest here are the linguistic conventions that structure the meanings assigned to disability and the patterns of response to disability that emanate from, or are attendant upon, those meanings.

The medical meaning-making was negotiated among interested parties who packaged their version of disability in ways that increased the ideas' potency and marketability. The disability community has attempted to wrest control of the language from the previous owners, and reassign meaning to the terminology used to describe disability and disabled people. This new language conveys different meanings, and, significantly, the shifts serve as metacommunications about the social, political, intellectual, and ideological transformations that have taken place over the past two decades.

NAMING OPPRESSION

It has been particularly important to bring to light language that reinforces the dominant culture's views of disability. A useful step in that process has been the construction of the terms *ableist* and *ableism*, which can be used to organize ideas about the centering and domination of the nondisabled experience and point of view. *Ableism* has recently landed in the *Reader's Digest Oxford Wordfinder* (Tulloch 1993), where it is defined as "discrimination in favor of the able-bodied." I would add, extrapolating from the definitions of *racism* and *sexism*, that *ableism* also includes the idea that a person's abilities or characteristics are determined by disability or that people with disabilities as a group are inferior to nondisabled people. Although there is probably greater consensus among the general public on what could be labeled racist or sexist language than there is on what might be considered ableist, that may be because the nature of the oppression of disabled people is not yet as widely understood.

NAMING THE GROUP

Across the world and throughout history various terminologies and meanings are ascribed to the types of human variations known in contemporary Westernized countries as disabilities. Over the past century the term *disabled* and others, such as *handicapped* and the less inclusive term *crippled*, have emerged as collective nouns that convey the idea that there is something that links this disparate group of people. The terms have been used to arrange people in ways that are socially and economically convenient to the society.

There are various consequences of the chosen terminology and variation in the degree of control that the named group has over the labeling process. The terms *disability* and *disabled people* are the most commonly used by disability rights activists, and recently policy makers and health care professionals have begun to use these terms more consistently. Although there is some agreement on terminology, there are disagreements about what it is that unites disabled people and whether disabled people should have control over the naming of their experience.

The term *disability*, as it has been used in general parlance, appears to signify something material and concrete, a physical or psychological condition considered to have predominantly medical significance. Yet it is an arbitrary designation, used erratically both by professionals who lay claim to naming such phenomena and by confused citizens. A project of disability studies scholars and the disability rights movement has been to bring into sharp relief the processes by which *disability* has been imbued with the meaning(s) it has and to reassign a meaning that is consistent with a sociopolitical analysis of disability. Divesting it of its current meaning is no small feat. As typically used, the term *disability* is a linchpin in a complex web of social ideals, institutional structures, and government policies. As a result, many people have a vested interest in keeping a tenacious hold on the current meaning because it is consistent with the practices and policies that are central to their livelihood or their ideologies. People may not be driven as much by economic imperatives as by a personal investment in their own beliefs and practices, in metaphors they hold dear, or in their own professional roles. Further, underlying this tangled web of needs and beliefs, and central to the arguments presented in this book is an epistemological structure that both generates and reflects current interpretations.[1]

A glance through a few dictionaries will reveal definitions of disability that include incapacity, a disadvantage, deficiency, especially a physical or mental impairment that restricts normal achievement; something that hinders or incapacitates, something that incapacitates or disqualifies. Legal definitions include legal incapacity or disqualification. *Stedman's Medical Dictionary* (1976) identifies *disability* as a "medicolegal term signifying loss of function and earning power," whereas *disablement* is a "medicolegal term signifying loss of function without loss of earning power" (400). These definitions are understood by the general public and by many in the academic community to be useful ones. *Disability* so defined is a medically derived term that assigns predominantly medical significance and meaning to certain types of human variation.

The decision to assign medical meanings to *disability* has had many and varied consequences for disabled people. One clear benefit has been the medical treatments that have increased the well-being and vitality of many disabled people, indeed have saved people's lives. Ongoing attention by the medical profession to the health and well-being of people with disabilities and to prevention of disease and impairments is critical. Yet, along with these benefits, there are enormous negative consequences that will take a large part of this book to list and explain. Briefly, the medicalization of disability casts human variation as deviance from the norm, as pathological condition, as deficit, and, significantly, as an individual burden and personal tragedy. Society, in agreeing to assign medical meaning to *disability,* colludes to keep the issue within the purview of the medical establishment, to keep it a personal matter and "treat" the condition and the person with the condition rather than "treating" the social processes and policies that constrict disabled people's lives. The disability studies' and disability rights movement's position is critical of the domination of the medical definition and views it as a major stumbling block to the reinterpretation of *disability* as a political category and to the social changes that could follow such a shift.

While retaining the term *disability*, despite its medical origins, a premise of most of the literature in disability studies is that *disability* is best understood as a marker of identity. As such, it has been used to build a coalition of people with significant impairments, people with behavioral or anatomical characteristics marked as deviant, and people who have or are suspected of having conditions, such as AIDS or emotional illness, that make them targets of discrimination.[2] As rendered in disability studies scholarship, disability has become a more capacious category, incorporating people with a range of physical, emotional, sensory, and cognitive conditions. Although the category is broad, the term is used to designate a specific minority group. When medical definitions of *disability* are dominant, it is logical to separate people according to biomedical condition through the use of diagnostic categories and to forefront medical perspectives on human variation. When disability is redefined as a social/political category, people with a variety of conditions are identified as *people with disabilities* or *disabled people,* a group bound by common social and political experience. These designations, as reclaimed by the community, are used to identify us as a constituency, to serve our needs for unity and identity, and to function as a basis for political activism.

The question of who "qualifies" as disabled is as answerable or as confounding as questions about any identity status. One simple response might be that you are disabled if you say you are. Although that declaration won't satisfy a worker's compensation board, it has a certain credibility with the disabled community. The degree and significance of an individual's impairment is often less of an issue than the degree to which someone identifies as disabled. Another way to answer the question is to say that disability "is mostly a social distinction . . . a marginalized status" and the status is assigned by "the majority culture tribunal" (Gill 1994, 44). But the problem gets stickier when the distinction between disabled and nondisabled is challenged by people who say,

"Actually, we're all disabled in some way, aren't we?" (46). Gill says the answer is no to those whose difference "does *not* significantly affect daily life and the person does not [with some consistency] present himself/herself to the world at large as a disabled person" (46). I concur with Gill; I am not willing or interested in erasing the line between disabled and nondisabled people, as long as disabled people are devalued and discriminated against, and as long as naming the category serves to call attention to that treatment.

Over the past twenty years, disabled people have gained greater control over these definitional issues. *The disabled* or *the handicapped* was replaced in the mid-70s by *people with disabilities* to maintain disability as a characteristic of the individual, as opposed to the defining variable. At the time, some people would purposefully say *women and men with disabilities* to provide an extra dimension to the people being described and to deneuter the way *the disabled* were traditionally described. Beginning in the early 90s *disabled people* has been increasingly used in disability studies and disability rights circles when referring to the constituency group. Rather than maintaining disability as a secondary characteristic, *disabled* has become a marker of the identity that the individual and group wish to highlight and call attention to.

In this book, the terms *disabled* and *nondisabled* are used frequently to designate membership within or outside the community. Disabled is centered, and nondisabled is placed in the peripheral position in order to look at the world from the inside out, to expose the perspective and expertise that is silenced. Occasionally, *people with disabilities* is used as a variant of *disabled people*. The use of *nondisabled* is strategic: to center disability. Its inclusion in this chapter is also to set the stage for postulating about the nondisabled position in society and in scholarship in later chapters. This action is similar to the strategy of marking and articulating "whiteness." The assumed position in scholarship has always been the male, white, nondisabled scholar; it is the default category. As recent scholarship has shown, these positions are not only presumptively hegemonic because they are the assumed universal stance, as well as the presumed neutral or objective stance, but also undertheorized. The nondisabled stance, like the white stance, is veiled. "*White* cannot be said quite out loud, or it loses its crucial position as a precondition of vision and becomes the object of scrutiny" (Haraway 1989, 152). Therefore, centering the disabled position and labeling its opposite nondisabled focuses attention on both the structure of knowledge and the structure of society. ·

NICE WORDS

Terms such as *physically challenged,* the *able disabled, handicapable,* and *special people/children* surface at different times and ·places. They are rarely used by disabled activists and scholars (except with palpable irony). Although they may be considered well-meaning attempts to inflate the value of people with disabilities, they convey the boosterism and do-gooder mentality endemic to the paternalistic agencies that control many disabled people's lives.

Physically challenged is the only term that seems to have caught on. Nondisabled· people use it in conversation around disabled people with no hint of anxiety, suggesting that they believe it is a positive term. This phrase does not make much sense to me. To say that I am physically challenged is to state that the obstacles to my participation are physical, not social, and that the barrier is my own disability. Further, it separates those of us with mobility impairments from other disabled people, not a valid or useful partition for those interested in coalition building and social change. Various derivatives of the term *challenged* have been adopted as a description used in jokes. For instance, "vertically challenged" is considered a humorous way to say short, and "calorically challenged" to say fat. A review of the Broadway musical *Big* in the *New Yorker* said that the score is "melodically challenged."

I observed a unique use of *challenged* in the local Barnes and Nobles superstore. The children's department has a section for books on "Children with Special Needs." There are shelves labeled "Epilepsy" and "Down Syndrome." A separate shelf at the bottom is labeled "Misc. Challenges," indicating that it is now used as an organizing category.

The term *able disabled* and *handicapable* have had a fairly short shelf life. They are used, it seems, to refute common stereotypes of incompetence. They are, though, defensive and reactive terms rather than terms that advance a new agenda.

An entire profession, in fact a number of professions, are built around the word *special*. A huge infrastructure rests on the idea that *special children* and *special education* are valid and useful structuring ideas. Although dictionaries insist that *special* be reserved for things that surpass what is common, are distinct among others of their kind, are peculiar to a specific person, have a limited or specific function, are arranged for a particular purpose, or are arranged for a particular occasion, experience teaches us that *special* when applied to education or to children means something different.

The naming of disabled children and the education that "is designed for students whose learning needs cannot be met by a standard school curriculum" (*American Heritage Dictionary* 1992) as *special* can be understood only as a euphemistic formulation, obscuring the reality that neither the children nor the education are considered desirable and that they are not thought to "surpass what is common."

Labeling the education and its recipients special may have been a deliberate attempt to confer legitimacy on the educational practice and to prop up a discarded group. It is also important to consider the unconscious feelings such a strategy may mask. It is my feeling that the nation in general responds to disabled people with great ambivalence. Whatever antipathy and disdain is felt is in competition with feelings of empathy, guilt, and identification. The term *special* may be evidence not of a deliberate maneuver but of a collective "reaction formation," Freud's term for the unconscious defense mechanism in which an individual adopts attitudes and behaviors that are opposite to his or her own true feelings, in order to protect the ego from the anxiety felt from experiencing the real feelings.

The ironic character of the word *special* has been captured in the routine on *Saturday Night Live*, where the character called the "Church Lady" declares when she encounters something distasteful or morally repugnant, "Isn't that special!"

NASTY WORDS

Some of the less subtle or more idiomatic terms for disabled people such as: *cripple, vegetable, dumb, deformed, retard,* and *gimp* have generally been expunged from public conversation but emerge in various types of discourse. Although they are understood to be offensive or hurtful, they are still used in jokes and in informal conversation.

Cripple as a descriptor of disabled people is considered impolite, but the word has retained its metaphoric vitality, as in "the exposé in the newspaper crippled the politician's campaign." The term is also used occasionally for its evocative power. A recent example appeared in *Lingua Franca* in a report on research on the behaviors of German academics. The article states that a professor had "documented the postwar careers of psychiatrists and geneticists involved in gassing thousands of cripples and schizophrenics" (Allen 1996, 37). *Cripple* is used rather loosely here to describe people with a broad range of disabilities. The victims of Nazi slaughter were people with mental illness, epilepsy, chronic illness, and mental retardation, as well as people with physical disabilities. Yet *cripple* is defined as "one that is partially disabled or unable to use a limb or limbs" (*American Heritage Dictionary* 1992) and is usually used only to refer to people with mobility impairments. Because *cripple* inadequately and inaccurately describes the group, the author of the report is likely to have chosen this term for its effect.

Cripple has also been revived by some in the disability community who refer to each other as "crips" or "cripples." A performance group with disabled actors call themselves the "Wry Crips." "In reclaiming 'cripple,' disabled people are taking the thing in their identity that scares the outside world the most and making it a cause to revel in with militant self-pride" (Shapiro 1993, 34).

A recent personal ad in the *Village Voice* shows how "out" the term is:

> **TWISTED CRIP:** Very sexy, full-figured disabled BiWF artist sks fearless, fun, oral BiWF for hot, no-strings nights. Wheelchair, tattoo, dom. Shaved a + N/S. No men/sleep-overs.

Cripple, gimp, and *freak* as used by the disability community have transgressive potential. They are personally and politically useful as a means to comment on oppression because they assert our right to name experience.

SPEAKING ABOUT OVERCOMING AND PASSING

The popular phrase *overcoming a disability* is used most often to describe someone with a disability who seems competent and successful in some way, in a sentence something like "She has overcome her disability and is a great success." One interpretation of the phrase might be that the individual's disability no longer limits her or him, that sheer strength or willpower has brought the person to the point where the disability is no longer a hindrance. Another implication of the phrase may be that the person has risen above society's expectation for someone with those characteristics. Because it is physically impossible to *overcome* a disability, it seems that what is *overcome* is the social stigma of having a disability. This idea is reinforced by the equally confounding statement "I never think of you as disabled." An implication of these statements is that the other members of the group from which the individual has supposedly moved beyond are not as brave, strong, or extraordinary as the person who has *overcome* that designation.

The expression is similar in tone to the phrase that was once more commonly used to describe an African American who was considered exceptional in some way: "He/she is a credit to his/her race." The implication of this phrase is that the "race" is somehow discredited and needs people with extraordinary talent to give the group the credibility that it otherwise lacks. In either case, talking about the person who is African American or talking about the person with a disability, these phrases are often said with the intention of complimenting someone. The compliment has a double edge. To accept it, one must accept the implication that the group is inferior and that the individual is unlike others in that group.

The ideas imbedded in the *overcoming* rhetoric are of personal triumph over a personal condition. The idea that someone can *overcome* a disability has not been generated within the community; it is a wish fulfillment generated from the outside. It is a demand that you be plucky and resolute, and not let the obstacles get in your way. If there are no curb cuts at the corner of the street so that people who use wheelchairs can get across, then you should learn to do wheelies and jump the curbs. If there are no sign language interpreters for deaf students at the high school, then you should study harder, read lips, and stay up late copying notes from a classmate. When disabled people internalize the demand to "overcome" rather than demand social change, they shoulder the same kind of exhausting and self-defeating "Super Mom" burden that feminists have analyzed.

The phrase *overcome a disability* may also be a shorthand version of saying "someone with a disability overcame many obstacles."

Tremblay (1996) uses that phrase when describing behaviors of disabled World War II veterans upon returning to the community: "[T]heir main strategies were to develop individualized strategies to overcome the obstacles they found in the community" (165). She introduces this idea as a means to describe how the vets relied on their own ingenuity to manage an inaccessible environment rather than demand that the community change to include them.

In both uses of *overcome*, the individual's responsibility for her or his own success is paramount. If we, as a society, place the onus on individuals with disabilities to work harder to "compensate" for their disabilities or to "overcome" their condition or the barriers in the environment, we have no need for civil rights legislation or affirmative action.

Lest I be misunderstood, I don't see working hard, doing well, or striving for health, fitness, and well-being as contradictory to the aims of the disability rights movement. Indeed, the movement's goal is to provide greater opportunity to pursue these activities. However, we shouldn't be impelled to do these because we have a disability, to prove to some social overseer that we can perform, but we should pursue them because they deliver their own rewards and satisfactions.

A related concept, familiar in African American culture as well as in lesbian and gay culture, is that of *passing*. African Americans who pass for white and lesbians and gays who pass for straight do so for a variety of personal, social, and often economic reasons. Disabled people, if they are able to conceal their impairment or confine their activities to those that do not reveal their disability, have been known to pass. For a member of any of these groups, passing may be a deliberate effort to avoid discrimination or ostracism, or it may be an almost unconscious, Herculean effort to deny to oneself the reality of one's racial history, sexual feelings, or bodily state. The attempt may be a deliberate act to protect oneself from the loathing of society or may be an unchecked impulse spurred by an internalized self-loathing. It is likely that often the reasons entail an admixture of any of these various parts.

Henry Louis Gates, Jr. (1996) spoke of the various reasons for passing in an essay on the literary critic Anatole Broyard. Broyard was born in New Orleans to a family that identified as "Negro." His skin was so light that for his entire career as "one of literary America's foremost gatekeepers" (66) the majority of people who knew him did not know this. His children, by then adults, learned of his racial history shortly before he died. Sandy Broyard, Anatole's wife, remarked that she thought that "his own personal history continued to be painful to him. . . . In passing, you cause your family great anguish, but I also think conversely, do we look at the anguish it causes the person who is passing? Or the anguish that it was born out of?" (75).

When disabled people are able to pass for nondisabled, and do, the emotional toll it takes is enormous. I have heard people talk about hiding a hearing impairment to classmates or colleagues for years, or others who manage to conceal parts of their body, or to hide a prosthesis. These actions, though, may not result in a family's anguish; they may, in fact, be behaviors that the family insists upon, reinforces, or otherwise shames the individual into. Some disabled people describe how they were subjected to numerous painful surgeries and medical procedures when they were young not so much, they believe, to increase their comfort and ease of mobility as to fulfill their families' wish to make them appear "more normal."

Even when a disability is obvious and impossible to hide on an ongoing basis, families sometimes create minifictions that disabled people are forced to play along with. Many people have told me that when family pictures were taken as they were growing up, they were removed from their wheelchairs, or they were shown only from the waist up, or they were excluded from pictures altogether.

The messages are that this part of you, your disability or the symbol of disability, your wheelchair, is unacceptable, or, in the last case, you are not an acceptable member of the family.

I was recently in an elementary school when class pictures were taken, and I learned that it is the custom for all the children who use wheelchairs to be removed from their chairs and carried up a few steps to the auditorium stage and placed on folding chairs. I spoke with people at the school who said they have thought about raising money to build a ramp to the stage, but in the meantime this was the solution. I wondered, of course, why they have to take pictures on the stage when it is inaccessible. The families of these children or the school personnel might even persist with this plan, believing that these actions have a positive effect on children, that they demonstrate that the disabled child is "just like everybody else." But these fictions are based more clearly on the projections of the adults than on the unadulterated feelings of the child. The message that I read in this action: You are like everyone else, but only as long as you hide or minimize your disability.

Both passing and overcoming take their toll. The loss of community, the anxiety, and the self-doubt that inevitably accompany this ambiguous social position and the ambivalent personal state are the enormous cost of declaring disability unacceptable. It is not surprising that disabled people also speak of "coming out" in the same way that members of the lesbian and gay community do. A woman I met at a disability studies conference not long ago said to me in the course of a conversation about personal experience: "I'm five years old." She went on to say that despite being significantly disabled for many years, she had really only recently discovered the disabled community and allied with it. For her, "coming out" was a process that began when she recognized how her effort to "be like everyone else" was not satisfying her own needs and wishes. She discovered other disabled people and began to identify clearly as disabled, and then purchased a motorized scooter, which meant she didn't have to expend enormous energy walking. She told this tale with gusto, obviously pleased with the psychic and physical energy she had gained. Stories such as hers provide evidence of the personal burdens many disabled people live with. Shame and fear are personal burdens, but if these tales are told, we can demonstrate how the personal is indeed the political. And further, that the unexamined connections between the personal and political are the curricular.

NORMAL/ABNORMAL

Normal and *abnormal* are convenient but problematic terms used to describe a person or group of people. These terms are often used to distinguish between people with and without disabilities. In various academic disciplines and in common usage, *normal* and *abnormal* assume different meanings. In psychometrics, *norm* or *normal* are terms describing individuals or characteristics that fall within the center of the normal distribution on whatever variable is being measured. However, as the notion of *normal* is applied in social science contexts and certainly in general parlance, it implies its obverse—*abnormal*—and they both become value laden. Often, those who are not deemed normal are devalued and considered a burden or problem, or are highly valued and regarded as a potential resource. Two examples are the variables of height and intelligence. Short stature and low measured intelligence are devalued and labeled abnormal, and people with those characteristics are considered disabled. Tall people (particularly males) and high scores on IQ tests are valued, and, although not normal in the statistical sense, are not labeled abnormal or considered disabled.[3]

Davis (1995) describes the historical specificity of the use of *normal* and thereby calls attention to the social structures that are dependent on its use. "[T]he very term that permeates our contemporary life—the normal—is a configuration that arises in a particular historical moment. It is part of a notion of progress, of industrialization, and of ideological consolidation of the power of the bourgeoisie. The implications of the hegemony of normalcy are profound and extend into the very heart of cultural production" (49).

The use of the terms *abnormal* and *normal* also moves discourse to a high level of abstraction, thereby avoiding concrete discussion of specific characteristics and increasing ambiguity in communication. In interactions, there is an assumed agreement between speaker and audience of what is normal that sets up an aura of empathy and "us-ness." This process "enhances social unity among those who feel they are normal" (Freilich, Raybeck, and Savishinsky 1991, 22), necessarily excluding the other or abnormal group.

These dynamics often emerge in discussions about disabled people when comparisons are made, for instance, between "the normal" and "the hearing impaired," or "the normal children" and "the handicapped children." The first example contrasts two groups of people; one defined by an abstract and evaluative term (the normal), the other by a more specific, concrete, and nonevaluative term (the hearing impaired). In the second comparison, the "handicapped children" are labeled abnormal by default. Setting up these dichotomies avoids concrete discussion of the ways the two groups of children actually differ, devalues the children with disabilities, and forces an "us and them" division of the population.

The absolute categories *normal* and *abnormal* depend on each other for their existence and depend on the maintenance of the opposition for their meaning. Sedgwick (1990), in *Epistemology of the Closet*, comments on a similar pattern in the forced choice categories homosexual and heterosexual:

> [C]ategories presented in a culture as symmetrical binary oppositions—heterosexual/homosexual, in this case—actually subsist in a more unsettled and dynamic tacit relation according to which, first, term B is not symmetrical with but subordinated to term

A; but, second, the ontologically valorized term A actually depends for its meaning on the simultaneous subsumption and exclusion of term B; hence, third, the question of priority between the supposed central and the supposed marginal category of each dyad is irresolvably unstable, an instability caused by the fact that term B is constituted as at once internal and external to term A. (9–10)

Despite the instability and the relational nature of the designations *normal* and *abnormal,* they are used as absolute categories. They have achieved their certainty by association with empiricism, and they suffer from empiricism's reductive and simplifying tendencies. Their power and reach are enormous. They affect individuals' most private deliberations about their worth and acceptability, and they determine social position and societal response to behavior. The relationship between abnormality and disability accords to the nondisabled the legitimacy and potency denied to disabled people. And, central to our concerns here, the reification of *normal* and *abnormal* structures curriculum. Courses with titles such as "Abnormal Psychology," "Sociology of Deviance," "Special Education," and "Psychopathology" assume the internal consistency of a curriculum focused on "the abnormal" and depend on the curriculum of the "normal" being taught elsewhere. In fact, this organization of knowledge implicitly suggests that the rest of the curriculum is "normal."

Rosemarie Garland Thomson (1997) has coined the term *the normate,* which, like *nondisabled,* is useful for marking the unexamined center. "This neologism names the veiled subject position of cultural self, the figure outlined by the array of deviant others whose marked bodies shore up the normate's boundaries. The term *normate* usefully designates the social figure through which people can represent themselves as definitive human beings" (8). By meeting *normal* on some of its own terms, *normate* inflects its root, and challenges the validity, indeed the possibility, of normal. At the same time, its ironic twist gives a more flavorful reading of the idea of normal.

PASSIVITY VERSUS CONTROL

Language that conveys passivity and victimization reinforces certain stereotypes when applied to disabled people. Some of the stereotypes that are particularly entrenched are that people with disabilities are more dependent, childlike, passive, sensitive, and miserable and are less competent than people who do not have disabilities. Much of the language used to depict disabled people relates the lack of control to the perceived incapacities, and implies that sadness and misery are the product of the disabling condition.

These deterministic and essentialist perspectives flourish in the absence of contradictory information. Historically, disabled people have had few opportunities to be active in society, and various social and political forces often undermine the capacity for self-determination. In addition, disabled people are rarely depicted on television, in films, or in fiction as being in control of their own lives—in charge or actively seeking out and obtaining what they want and need. More often, disabled people are depicted as pained by their fate or, if happy, it is through personal triumph over their adversity. The adversity is not depicted as lack of opportunity, discrimination, institutionalization, and ostracism; it is the personal burden of their own body or means of functioning.

Phrases such as *the woman is a victim of cerebral palsy* implies an active agent (cerebral palsy) perpetrating an aggressive act on a vulnerable, helpless "victim." The use of the term *victim*, a word typically used in the context of criminal acts, evokes the relationship between perpetrator and victim. Using this language attributes life, power, and intention to the condition and disempowers the person with the disability, rendering him or her helpless and passive. Instead, if there is a particular need to note what an individual's disability is, saying *the woman has cerebral palsy* describes solely the characteristic of importance to the situation, without imposing extraneous meaning.

Grover (1987) analyzes the word *victim* as used to describe people with AIDS. She notes that the term implies fatalism, and therefore "enable[s] the passive spectator or the AIDS 'spectacle' to remain passive." Use of the term may also express the unconscious wish that the people with AIDS may have been "complicit with, to have courted, their fate" (29), in which case the individual would be seen as a *victim* of her or his own drives. This is particularly apparent when the phrase *innocent victim* is used to distinguish those who acquire HIV from blood transfusions or other medical procedures from those who contract HIV from sexual contact or shared needles. This analysis is also pertinent to people with other disabilities because a number of belief systems consider disability, or some disabilities, as punishment for sin in this or a former life.

Disabled people are frequently described as *suffering from* or *afflicted with* certain conditions. Saying that someone is *suffering from* a condition implies that there is a perpetual state of suffering, uninterrupted by pleasurable moments or satisfactions. *Afflicted* carries similar assumptions. The verb *afflict* shares with *agonize, excruciate, rack, torment,* and *torture* the central meaning "to bring great harm or suffering to someone" (*American Heritage Dictionary* 1992, 30). Although some people may experience their disability this way, these terms are not used as descriptors of a verified experience but are projected onto disability. Rather than assume suffering in the description of the situation, it is more accurate and less histrionic to say simply that a person *has a disability*. Then, wherever it is relevant, describe the nature and extent of the difficulty experienced. My argument here isn't to eliminate descriptions of suffering but to be accurate in their appointment. It is interesting that AIDS activists intentionally use the phrase *living with AIDS* rather than *dying from AIDS*, not to deny the reality of AIDS but to emphasize that people are often actively engaged in living even in the face of a serious illness.

The ascription of passivity can be seen in language used to describe the relationship between disabled people and their wheelchairs. The phrases *wheelchair bound* or *confined to a wheelchair* are frequently seen in newspapers and magazines, and heard in conversation. A more puzzling variant was spotted in *Lingua Franca*, which described the former governor of Alabama, George Wallace, as the "slumped, wheelchair-ridden 'Guv'nah' " (Zalewski 1995, 19). The choice here was to paint the wheelchair user as *ridden*, meaning "dominated, harassed, or obsessed by" (*American Heritage Dictionary* 1992), rather than the rider in the wheelchair. The various terms imply that a wheelchair restricts the individual, holds a person prisoner. Disabled people are more likely to say that someone *uses a wheelchair*. The latter phrase not only indicates the active nature of the user and the positive way that wheelchairs increase mobility and activity but recognizes that people get in and out of wheelchairs for different activities: driving a car, going swimming, sitting on the couch, or, occasionally, for making love.

A recent oral history conducted with disabled Canadian World War II veterans and other disabled people who are contemporaries of the vets recounts their memories of the transition from hospital-style wicker wheelchairs used to transport patients to self-propelled, lighter-weight, folding chairs that were provided to disabled people, mostly to veterans, in the years following the war. Prior to the new chairs, one man recalls that "one was often confined to bed for long periods of time. . . . There were a few cerebral palsy chaps there. . . . If they transgressed any rule . . . they'd take their wheelchairs away from them and leave them in bed for two weeks" (Tremblay 1996, 153). In this and other interviews the value of wheelchairs is revealed. A vet described how the medical staff's efforts were geared toward getting veterans to walk with crutches, but when the vets discovered the self-propelled chairs they realized "it didn't make much sense spending all that energy covering a short distance [on crutches] . . . when you could do it quickly and easily with a wheelchair. . . . It didn't take long for people to get over the idea that walking was that essential" (158–59). Another veteran recalled how the staff's emphasis on getting the men to walk "delayed our rehabilitation for months and months" (159). The staff obviously understood the value of the wheelchair to disabled people; otherwise they would not have used it as a means of control, yet they resisted purchasing the new self-push chairs for some time after they were made available. It is that type of manipulation and control, along with architectural and attitudinal barriers, that confine people. It is not wheelchairs.

MULTIPLE MEANINGS

Are *invalid*, with the emphasis on the first syllable, and *invalid*, with the emphasis on the second, synonyms or homonyms? Does the identical housing of *patient*, the adjective, and *patient*, the noun, conflate the two meanings? Did their conceptual relationship initially determine their uniform casing?

For instance, *invalid* is a designation used to identify some disabled people. The term is seen most prominently on the sides of vans used to transport people with mobility impairments. Disabled people, desperate for accessible transportation, must use vans with the dubious appellation *"Invalid Coach"* printed in bold letters on the side. Aside from this being a fertile source of jokes about the aptness of these notoriously bad transportation services being identified as "not factually or legally valid; falsely based or reasoned; faulty" (*American Heritage Dictionary* 1992), those on the inside of the bus suffer the humiliation of being written off so summarily. Both *invalids* share the Latin root *invalidus*, which means weak. It could be argued that some disabilities do result in weakening of the body, or, more likely, parts of the body, but the totalizing noun, *invalid,* does not confine the weakness to the specific bodily functions; it is more encompassing.

The homonymic *patient/patient,* is, I think, not coincidental or irrelevant. The noun *patient* is a role designation that is always relational. A patient is understood to belong to a doctor or other health care professional, or more generally to an institution. As a noun, *patient* is a neutral description of the role of "one who receives medical attention, care, or treatment" (*American Heritage Dictionary* 1992). The adjective *patient* moves beyond the noun's neutral designation to describe a person who is capable of "bearing or enduring pain, difficulty, provocation, or annoyance with calmness" as well as "tolerant . . . persevering . . . constant . . . not hasty" (*American Heritage Dictionary* 1992). The "good" patient is one who does not challenge the authority of the practitioner or institution and who complies with the regimen set out by the expert, in other words a patient patient. Disabled people, who have often spent a great deal of time as patients, discuss the ways that we have been socialized in the medical culture to be compliant, and that has often undermined our ability to challenge authority or to function autonomously. Further, the description of disabled people as patients in situations where we are not, reinforces these ideas.[4]

REFLECTIONS ON THE *DIS* IN DISABILITY

Before discussing the prefix *dis,* let's examine a similar bound morpheme that conveys meaning and significantly modifies the words it is attached to. The suffix *ette,* when appended to nouns, forms words meaning small or diminutive, as in *kitchenette;* female, as in *usherette;* or imitation or inferior kind, as in *leatherette* (*American Heritage Dictionary* 1992). These various meanings of *ette* slip around in our minds to influence how we interpret other words with the same suffix. So, for instance, although the word *leatherette* is used to tell us it is not the real thing and an inferior version of leather, *usherette* becomes, by association, not only the female version of usher but denotes a poor imitation. *Usherette* becomes, like *kitchenette,* the diminutive version. These various meanings tumble into one another, propagating new meanings, unintended and imprecise. I recently met a woman who told me that she had been a Rockette at Radio City Music Hall in Rockefeller Center for twenty years. I realized that this string of high-kicking, synchronized dancing women are perpetually cast as the smaller, imitation, inferior and female counterparts of the great male barons, the Rockefellers.

The prefix *dis,* like the suffix *ette,* has similarly unchecked impulses. Although *ette* qualifies its base and reduces it to the more diminutive and less valid version, a relationship is maintained between the base and its amended version. However, the prefix *dis* connotes separation, taking apart, sundering in two. The prefix has various meanings such as not, as in *dissimilar;* absence of, as in *disinterest;* opposite of, as in *disfavor;* undo, do the opposite of, as in *disarrange;* and deprive of, as in *disfranchise.* The Latin root *dis* means apart, asunder. Therefore, to use the verb *disable,* means, in part, to deprive of capability or effectiveness. The prefix creates a barrier, cleaving in two ability and its absence, its opposite. Disability is the "not" condition, the repudiation of ability.

Canguilhem (1991), in his explorations of the normal and the pathological, recognizes the way that prefixes signal their relationship to the words they modify. He asserts that

> the pathological phenomena found in living organisms are nothing more than quantitative variations, greater or lesser according to corresponding physiological phenomena. Semantically, the pathological is designated as departing from the normal not so much by *a-* or *dys-* as by *hyper-* or *hypo-.* . . . [T]his approach is far from considering health and sickness as qualitatively opposed, or as forces joined in battle." (42)

Ette, hyper and *hypo,* and *dis* have semantic consequences, but, moreover, each recapitulates a particular social arrangement. The suffix *ette* not only qualifies the meaning of the root word it is attached to but speaks of the unequal yet dynamic relationship between women and men, in which "woman was, as we see in the profoundly influential works of Aristotle, not the equal opposite of man but a failed version of the supposedly defining type" (Minnich 1990, 54). The medical prefixes *hyper* and *hypo* are typically attached to medical conditions that are temporary or circumscribed. People with those conditions are not socially marked and separated as are those with the more pronounced, and long standing conditions known as disabilities. With *hyper* and *hypo* conditions, there is less semantic and social disjuncture. However, the construction of *dis/ability* does not imply the continuum approach Canguilhem finds in diagnostic categories. *Dis* is the semantic reincarnation of the split between disabled and nondisabled people in society.

Yet *women and men with disabilities, disabled people,* and the *disability community* are terms of choice for the group. We have decided to reassign meaning rather than choose a new name. In retaining *disability* we run the risk of preserving the medicalized ideas attendant upon it in most people's idea of disability. What I think will help us out of the dilemma is the naming of the political category in which *disability* belongs. Women is a category of *gender,* and black or Latino/a are categories of *race/ethnicity,* and it is the recognition of those categories that has fostered understanding of the political meaning of *women* and *black.* Although *race* and *gender* are not perfect terms because they retain biological meanings in many quarters, the categories are increasingly understood as axes of oppression; axes along which power and resources are distributed. Although those of us within the disability community recognize that power is distributed along disability lines, the naming and recognition of the axis will be a significant step in gaining broader recognition of the issues. Further, it will enrich the discussion of the intersections of the axes of class, race, gender and sexual orientation, and disability.

Constructing the axis on which disabled and nondisabled fall will be a critical step in marking all points along it. Currently, there is increased attention to the privileged points on the continua of race, gender, and sexual orientation. There is growing recognition that the white, the male, and the heterosexual positions need to be noted and theorized. Similarly, it is important to examine the nondisabled position and its privilege and power. It is not the neutral, universal position from which disabled people deviate, rather, it is a category of people whose power and cultural capital keep them at the center.

In this book, though, disabled people's perspectives are kept central and are made explicit, partly to comment on how marginal and obscure they typically are, and partly to suggest the disciplinary and intellectual transformation consequent on putting disability studies at the center.

NOTES

1. Various authors have discussed issues related to definitions of *disability*. See Wendell (1996), Longmore (1985b, 1987), and Hahn (1987), and also the June Isaacson Kailes (1995) monograph *Language Is More Than a Trivial Concern!* which is available from the Institute on Disability Culture, 2260 Sunrise Point Road, Las Cruces, New Mexico 88011.

2. The definition of *disability* under the Americans with Disabilities Act is consistent with the sociopolitical model employed in disability studies. A person is considered to have a disability if he or she:
   - has a physical or mental impairment that substantially limits one or more of his or her major life activities;

- has a record of such an impairment; or
- is regarded as having such an impairment.

The last two parts of this definition acknowledge that even in the absence of a substantially limiting impairment, people can be discriminated against. For instance, this may occur because someone has a facial disfigurement or has, or is suspected of having, HIV or mental illness. The ADA recognizes that social forces, such as myths and fears regarding disability, function to substantially limit opportunity.

3. I am indebted to my colleague John O'Neill for his input on these ideas about the use of the term *normal.*
4. See June Isaacson Kailes's (1995), *Language Is More Than a Trivial Concern!* for a discussion on language use.

DIVIDED SOCIETY

I have the right when I go out and pay good money for a meal to enjoy it. The sight of a woman in a wheelchair with food running down her chin would make me throw up. I believe my rights should be respected as much as the rights of the person in the wheelchair . . . maybe even more so, because I am normal and she is not.

In my opinion, restaurants should have a special section for handicapped people—partially hidden by palms or other greenery so they are not seen by other guests.

—excerpts from two letters printed
in an Ann Landers column, spring 1987

No person who is diseased, maimed, mutilated or in any way deformed so as to be an unsightly or disgusting object or improper person to be allowed in or on the public ways or other public places in this city, shall therein or thereon expose himself to public view, under penalty of not less than one dollar nor more than fifty dollars for each offense. —from the Municipal Code of the City of Chicago

It is in the formal and informal, the explicit and the tacit, the overt and the covert that society works to divide up the human community and oppress some of its members. The above example of public rules and private thoughts (revealed in the safety of anonymity) may not seem to have much force. Federal law prohibits such discrimination, and public expression of these sentiments would be scorned in many circles and the speakers branded as unsympathetic or uncharitable, not to mention unsophisticated. But the underlying ethos has not dissolved with shifting practices; it remains a virulent force with new manifestations.

As Young (1990) notes:

The objectification and overt domination of despised bodies that obtained in the nineteenth century, however, has receded in our time, and a discursive commitment to equality for all has emerged. Racism, sexism, homophobia, ageism, and ableism, I argue, have not disappeared with that commitment, but have gone underground, dwelling in everyday habits and cultural meanings of which people are for the most part unaware. (124)

To Young's comments I would add that in addition to the everyday habits and cultural meanings, there remain policies and practices that serve to control and marginalize disabled people. Unfortunately, these barriers to the integration of disabled people are often not fully visible, at least not to the untrained observer. They function like the "glass ceiling" that women come up against when attempting to advance in business. But it would be a mistake to say that the barriers that women or disabled people encounter are truly invisible. For instance, the policy to exclude women from private clubs where business deals are clinched might be made visible by looking at the bylaws of such clubs, or by testing the admissions practices. The practices within the clubs can be revealed by conducting research on the behaviors and habits of their members to find out how they transact business while seeming to talk about golf. Of course it would take extraordinary methods to expose all the structural inequities that exist in the business world and other significant arenas that privilege some groups' participation and success. Moreover, as Marx and others have instructed us, these local events are often controlled by forces beyond the purview of those acting at that site, making it even more difficult to gain access to the information (Gorelick 1996). Nevertheless, it is important to recognize that by calling the barriers invisible we run the

35

risk of implying that they are so amorphous and intangible that we can't document them and can't change them.

A watchful outsider might recognize some of the more obvious barriers that exclude disabled people from participation in society but may have the false impression that there are few hidden barriers. It may seem that if ramps are built to get into all the polling places, sign language interpreters are provided at public functions, and the Constitution is transcribed into Braille, we will have done away with the inequities. But redressing second-class citizenship, 66 percent unemployment, incarceration in institutions, and separate and unequal education will take more than these mechanical changes (Shapiro 1993).

Although an enormous amount of research is yet to be done to document the complex history of these practices and to catalogue their current manifestations, we can review what is already known about humans' response to disability to see that disability has been conceptualized and responded to in a variety of ways throughout history and across human cultures. It is not a singular history. There isn't, as some might imagine, a clear stream of progress from prehistory to the present moment. Nor is it accurate to valorize the United States and other Westernized countries for exemplary practices and an enlightened vision.

This chapter examines the variations in social arrangements that have existed throughout history and currently exist around the world. Of course, it is not possible to provide a complete history of humans' response to disability. Some significant examples have been chosen in order to demonstrate the variation and to expose some of the problems that have occurred in the documentation and interpretation of that history. Disabled people have existed predominantly as marginal figures, their contributions and perspectives are not generally noted. Researchers outside disability studies have not been actively interested in this history nor in examining the meaning and function of disability in the lives of the few well-known people with disabilities.

The disability history that does exist is heavily dominated by the perspectives of scholars from the United States and Western Europe, whether they are looking at their own country's practices or others', leaving even more obscure the perspectives from the remainder of the world. Further, these reports usually do not make differentiations along gender, class, or race lines; therefore, many of the statements made about "treatment of disabled people" are not truly for the whole population. The most fundamental problem, though, is that disabled people's voices are almost completely absent from this picture, and so the understanding of disabled people's place in these situations is filtered through the experience of people who have never been in that place.

VARIATIONS

Although there are variations across time and cultures in response to disability, there are patterns that can be traced. An article by Hanks and Hanks written in 1948 provides a useful starting point for organizing the available evidence into a typology or classification system. While their study, *The Physically Handicapped in Certain Non-Occidental Societies,* predates the formal presentation of social models of disability by some thirty years, it is focused on the social variables that structure participation of disabled people in selected societies. It is a strength of the report that they looked primarily *at* social participation rather than at treatment or care provided to disabled people, and that they looked *to* the social structure for the explanation of the degree of integration or participation of disabled people in each society rather than to the nature of the disability itself or the psychological makeup of disabled individuals. Astonishingly, they also in some instances point out class and gender differences in disability experience in instructive ways. There are also some limitations to their schema, to their interpretations, and to the data they looked to for evidence.

Hanks and Hanks analyzed practices in a number of cultures, with a particular interest in response to physical disability in "non-Occidental" societies. A limitation of their material, therefore, for the present analysis is that practices related to people with other disabilities are not included; relatively few countries were actually studied; and Westernized and/or industrialized countries are not included. The few gender and class differences they did note are inadequate to the complexity that exists, and, further, their descriptions fall short of the meaning that these differences have for the people they describe. Another limitation is that their conceptualization of response to disability into the five domains they chose limits the range of practices that can be studied. Therefore, I have added a sixth category and reworked some of the descriptive material to include an even broader range of data and more contemporary examples. In a number of places, I have indicated ways that a more explicit and differentiated scheme could be fashioned from the data and theoretical formulations that have emerged since their study. These caveats aside, the Hankses' original categories, Pariah, Economic Liability, Tolerant Utilization, Limited Participation, and Laissez-faire, as amended, are described below, along with the sixth category, Active Participation and Accommodation that I have added.

1. PARIAH

The first category, Pariah, is described by Hanks and Hanks (1948) as cultures in which disabled people are "denied all claims to succor by the protective group and [are] deemed a threat to the group itself" (13). I have amended this to read that disabled people are denied most if not all claims to succor and to rights by the dominant nondisabled majority and are deemed a threat to the group itself. This revision alters the category in three significant ways. The addition of "rights" and "dominant group" makes explicit the power differentials in these situations in which nondisabled people determine what resources, if any, will be made available to disabled people. I have eliminated the Hankses' term "protective group" because it assumes that protection is the desired behavior. Although the definition of *pariah* in many dictionaries is solely "social outcast," typical usage and other dictionaries also incorporate more active and virulent meanings, such as Merriam Webster's "despised by society." Throughout history there have been groups whose religious beliefs or social customs sanctioned practices that were harmful, and often lethal, for disabled people. Therefore, the practices discussed in this category reflect more than the passive meaning, that the individual is an outcast; rather, the examples support the stance of "casting out" or harming these despised members of society.

Denying or withholding resources or protection is one set of responses to disabled people deemed pariahs. Hanks and Hanks (1948) state that the practice of denying all protection and care is "most frequent in India" (13), where the family is put at risk by having a disabled member because its social position is thereby threatened. The family may deny the individual protection. However, a woman is told to care for, indeed worship, her disabled husband even if his family abandons him. Women with disabilities, it seems, would not expect the reciprocal response from their husbands.

Directly harming or killing disabled people is an even more aggressive means of managing the perceived threat. It is ironic that the Hankses, writing in the late 1940s, pointed toward India, when evidence of what was probably the most comprehensive example of systematic violence toward disabled people was known. Granted their focus was on "non-Occidental" societies, but they wrote "most frequent in India" and other phrases in an absolute manner, implying its unequivocal status. Nazi Germany took specific actions to eliminate disabled people and succeeded in annihilating 200,000 "disabled men, women and children . . . 'Lebensunwertes Leben'—life unworthy of life—was the concept Nazi doctors used to justify their practice of direct medical euthanasia" (Shapiro 1993, 271). Disabled people threatened the idea of Aryan perfection, constructed around a very narrow band of acceptable behavior, appearance, and genetic makeup. (The contributions of the United States to the early eugenics movement on which Nazi practices were built is discussed in the next chapter.)

A most profound example of withholding care and "succor" can be seen in the United States, in the history of many of our institutions and asylums. In the early 1970s Geraldo Rivera described the conditions at the Willowbrook State School that were "not unlike Nazi deathcamps. At Willowbrook, Rivera told his viewers, one hundred percent of all residents contracted hepatitis within six months of entering the institution. . . . Many lay on dayroom floors (naked) in their own feces" (Trent 1994, 258). A more recent example, affecting people with a broader range of disabilities, is reported by Asch and Fine (1988, 23) from a *New York Times* article from 1984. "An inquiry into California's community care facilities for the mentally and physically disabled and for the elderly found that 'daily, throughout the state, residents of community care facilities are being sexually abused, beaten, fed spoiled food, forced to live with toilets that don't work.' "

There are varying reports on the degree to which infanticide has occurred in the past or still does. Scheer and Groce (1988) note that infanticide of disabled newborns is not commonly practiced in developing countries, despite popular beliefs to the contrary. However, a number of examples of disabled children being killed at birth or shortly thereafter have been documented. These practices, though, also target children not considered disabled by Western definitions, such as babies with extra fingers or twins. For instance, Nichols (1993) reports that among the Ashantis of central Ghana infants with six fingers are killed at birth and with "the Igbo and some other groups infanticide sometimes occurred following the birth of twins" (32).

Mallory (1993) describes how the Songye tribe of Zaire divides all children with physical anomalies into three categories: ceremonial, miserable, or faulty. "Miserable children are those born with albinism, dwarfism, or hydrocephaly." They are not seen as human beings; rather, they are thought to be supernatural beings and are accorded "an inferior status in the tribe, and little is done to make their lives comfortable or meaningful" (18). The Igide of Nigeria are reported to "tolerate" certain "minor birth defects" but other "abnormal babies are usually killed and thrown away by the Ebih priest" (Nichols 1993, 32). The practice of "throwing away," or abandoning babies on river banks or in the bush, is practiced by the Igbo with twins and by the Ashantis with "severely" retarded infants because both groups of infants are thought to be animal-like. Whyte (1995) reports that these practices have tapered off in recent times and that there is increased conflict between the parents, who often wish to have the infant live, and the will of the elders of the tribe, who may wish to conform to ritual practices. Ross (1983) reports that "infanticide in hunting and gathering societies was probably universally practiced in instances of congenital birth defects" and also notes that there are "ethnographic references to the ritual disposal of adolescents and adults when they had become physically disabled and were unable to be ambulatory or fulfill certain tasks." Ross later says that these actions are taken "only when selective pressures were beyond the control of the particular group in question" (137).

A recent report in the *Atlantic Monthly* on orphanages in China demonstrates how vulnerable babies born with disabilities are there. It should be noted that other infants are also vulnerable in those institutions, particularly girls. Anne Thurston (1996) reported that for years friends had been telling her "that severely handicapped infants—those with incapacitating infirmities requiring full-time care—are routinely allowed to die" (40). Other infants are placed in "dying rooms" as well, although it appears that the practice is more systematic and probably more generally accepted when the infants are disabled. A doctor with whom Thurston spoke, "a man of great compassion," pointed out that the "best of his people have suffered the most egregious persecution. . . [therefore] does it not follow that those of so little official worth—the handicapped and abandoned—should be allowed to die" (40). This statement is Thurston's paraphrase, and hence it is not possible to tell whether the word "official" as a modifier of "worth" is the doctor's view, Thurston's, or the government's. However, "the best of his people" is said straightforwardly and implies its opposite, the worst. Comments such as these come out in public unchecked when the speaker assumes that there is consensus on the official worth of disabled people.

In the reports of Chinese and African practices, a number of explanations are provided for these practices that emanate from commonly held belief systems. For instance, the Buddhist belief that "a severe handicap [is] . . . evidence of a heinous crime in a previous life" and the Confucian belief that "a severely handicapped child would be incapable of fulfilling the immutable demands of filial piety and thus unable to behave as a proper human being" (Thurston 1996, 40) are mentioned. Nichols, in discussing the derivations of African practices, makes an important distinction between beliefs that emerge from what he calls *"pragmatic spirituality"* and those attributable to *"blind superstition"* (1993, 29). His objective is to take a more serious look at belief systems that have often been dismissed as "primitive" or "barbaric" and to demonstrate the humanitarian and practical responses evidenced in African cultures. It is ironic, and unfortunate, that a metaphoric use of *blind* is employed in this context, particularly because, in contrast to pragmatic spirituality, which is thought to reflect knowledge and utility, blind superstition is in "bondage to ignorance" (29). All these pragmatic and metaphysical explanations provide useful material for analysis, but a rigorous examination of the practices themselves needs to be made. Ritual "disposal" of disabled people and infanticide are murder and therefore individual acts, no matter what function they are serving and no matter what complex longstanding imperatives they fulfill.

The recent debates about euthanasia, currently being called "physician-assisted suicide," and about prenatal screening and selective abortion in North America and in Europe have raised concerns about the "right to life" of disabled people. The Supreme Court in the United States is deliberating on the legality of physician-assisted suicide, and the issue is being debated throughout the press. Disabled people and allies, in demonstrations outside the Court in January 1996 and in other fora, have been pointing out that "suicide" implies a fully voluntary act, and for many disabled people and poor people there are coercive forces that act on their choices. Particularly in the climate of managed care, where the economic imperatives that guide a physician's choices are increasingly powerful, the supposed "expense" of disabled people's lives make us more vulnerable to coercion. Further, physicians are not reliable judges of the value and worth of disabled people's lives. Nat Hentoff (1997b) reports that Dr. Katherine Foley, cochief of the Pain and Palliative Care Service at the Memorial Sloan-Kettering Cancer Center, said in an interview that "physicians consistently underestimate the quality of living for those individuals who are disabled."

For a number of years disabled people have been watching the Netherlands, where "Dutch doctors have been empowered to help patients kill themselves, and, increasingly, physicians there have been directly killing patients without being asked to" (Hentoff 1997a). Hentoff asked a television interviewer how the "Dutch people can justify not only this 'quality of life' killing of adults, which brings back memories of Nazi occupiers—but also the liquidating of 'defective' children." It is particularly horrible that today the Dutch appear complicit in these actions when just over fifty years ago, Dutch physicians gave up their medical licenses rather then join the Nazi medical association. A study conducted in 1995 revealed that "23 percent of the doctors interviewed reported that they had euthanized a patient without his or her explicit request," and in some cases made the initial suggestion that "death should be embraced."

Less egregious than murder but socially and personally devastating is the practice of ostracizing and vilifying members of a society. Two recent reports from Japan provide examples of behaviors that have existed and continue in many places in the world. The headline of a *New York Times* article by N. D. Kristof (1996) declares, "Outcast Status Worsens Pain of Japan's Disabled." Osamu Takahashi, now age forty-nine and the director of a center for disabled people in Japan, told the reporter that

> [he] never went to any school and was hidden in the house from birth until the age of 26. While the rest of his family ate together, he was served meals alone in his room. His family allowed him out of the house only about once a year, and then mostly at night so the neighbors would not see . . . [and] that view still survives in some households. (3)

The term *outcast* seems to have particular saliency for disabled people in Japan. Other people interviewed for the article described discrimination in housing, education, and employment but emphasized the pain and frustration of being social outcasts. S. Sesser (1994) reported in the *New Yorker* on the particularly painful experience that people who are HIV positive have in Japan. "With the sick and the disabled ordinarily feeling like outcasts, it's not surprising that those Japanese infected with H.I.V. are the most reclusive of all" (64).

Disabled people around the world who are deemed pariahs by their own families and communities have lived through the terrible pain of being denied succor by the very persons to whom it would be most natural to turn. Practices ranging from withholding attention, food, love, and education to denying them life itself have been documented. For the most part the practices described here are not unique to that particular culture. Many disabled people around the globe have stories to tell of abuse and marginalization. As the rest of this chapter will demonstrate, casting out and vilifying disabled people is the extreme end of a long and complex continuum.

2. ECONOMIC AND SOCIAL LIABILITY

I've changed the Hanks and Hanks (1948) original category, Economic Liability, to Economic and Social Liability to permit inclusion of examples of disabled people's being seen as impairing the economic well-being, as well as the vitality and viability, of a society. Even if disabled people are not considered pariahs, those who are thought to bring harm directly to individuals or to the group, there are situations or cultures where disabled people are unwelcome because they are thought to drain resources or deflect attention from other needs. Included in this category are the more extreme examples, couched in survivalist rhetoric, that invoke a lifeboat image of a society abandoning the "weaker" members to aid the survival of the group. Responses to these imperatives range from containment and control to abandonment and annihilation, all enacted ostensibly to conserve resources and protect the interests of the majority. This section does not survey practices across different countries but, rather, traces liability themes by describing the emergence of modern approaches to disability from the seventeenth through twentieth centuries in the United States and Europe.

The modernist "solution" to disability was the institutionalization of disabled people and the medicalization of all responses to disability. These were understood to be benchmarks of progress in the modern era. There are at least two competing ideas at work here. One is the belief that in the modern, industrialized world scientific and technological competence, coupled with advanced humanitarian and moral development, would lead the way toward the highest level of care and of concern ever evidenced. However, those modernist ideals mean the society would not tolerate being bogged down by those who can't keep up, who are thought to drain resources, or who remind us in any way of the limitations of our scientific capabilities. In both ideas, the issues of efficiency prevail, leading to actions taken to contain the perceived negative social and economic impact of disability on society, even when glossed with an altruistic facade.

In the early years of the founding of the United States, and during a similar time frame in Europe, there were few facilities where disabled people were housed or cared for in systematic ways. Disabled people lived in their communities and occupied roles ranging from shoemaker to town fool to despised outcast. Their roles and degree of acceptance depended on a number of factors, including type of community, whether rural or urban; nature of the disability; status of the family; and gender, race, or personality of the individual. Paul Starr (1982) writes that "in the colonial period, the mentally ill, along with other classes of dependents, were treated as a local responsibility, primarily within their own or other families" (72). Early in the history of this country, individuals who would today be labeled mentally retarded were absorbed into communities with varying degrees of acceptance and support. Before the advent of large institutions, there were a few places, such as convents, where groups of disabled people were housed. What is apparent is that whatever ways disabled people were accommodated, the response was local and informal. For some disabled people, these situations were relatively comfortable. However, because of the idiosyncratic and arbitrary nature of these accommodations, disabled people were more likely to be ostracized than they were to be functioning members of the community. Further, even if work and participation in religious activities were possible, they may not have had opportunities for friendship, love, and intimacy. More systematic responses were to come, with varying outcomes for disabled people.

From the seventeenth through the twentieth centuries, a number of economic and philosophical factors affected community life for disabled people. Fraser and Gordon (1994) describe a transformation in policies for those in need and, moreover, in the whole idea of "dependency." America imported from England the model social legislation embodied in the Poor Relief Act of 1601 and it "did more than influence American laws—for the first 150 years of the colonies' existence, it was American law" (Groce 1992, 7). The act acknowledged a responsibility to "disabled in need" but with a clear distinction made between those who were deemed worthy of such help and those who were not (7–8). The act may have given some disabled people more consistent financial support and relieved families of some financial responsibilities, but it also functioned to make more rigid the dividing lines between those for whom dependency was "deemed natural and proper" and those for whom receiving assistance was a source of shame.

During the seventeenth century, dependency on public assistance became more stigmatized. Whereas in the early days of the colonies "dependency" was considered a social relationship between one group and another, for instance, between workers and landowners, increasingly "*dependency* could also designate an individual character trait" (Fraser and Gordon 1994, 315). A differentiated reading of dependency along gender and race lines emerged: women and the "dark races" were deemed acceptable as dependents, but it was considered shameful for white males to accept public assistance. Further, "dependency was deemed antithetical to citizenship" (315), which was also related to race and gender, and to disability. The condition of dependency was considered acceptable by the dominant majority for some groups, but it deprived recipients of the rights of citizenship and forced people to appear helpless in order to insure continued receipt of benefits.

America's glorification of independence has not served disabled people well. Individual worth came to be increasingly judged in terms of financial and social independence, a goal very, very few disabled people, nonwhites, and women could reach.

In the nineteenth century, there was a shift from the belief that disability was caused by supernatural agency[1] to a biological explanation that held that treatment, or some form of rehabilitation, was the logical response to disability (Longmore 1987). That shift marked the birth of an enormous "care" industry and along with it a variety of institutions, asylums, and state schools. Following the Civil War, a more comprehensive generalized approach to dealing with people in need of support developed that took the financial burden off families and communities. Trent (1994) reports, "[T]he shift from local to state responsibility for many groups of the disabled poor—the mad, the blind, the deaf, and the delinquent—[and] care for feebleminded people became part of a response to rapid changes in the social and economic fabric of American life" (39). Contributing to medical and state intervention were the growth of cities and the mobility of families. The population density in cities resulted in "a higher concentration of the insane . . . and a greater demand for order and security" (Starr 1982, 72). Trent also traces the development of a medicalized response to people with mental retardation in the United States and the birth of orphanages, asylums, and state-operated schools. These appeared throughout the country in the early eighteenth century; however, most would not admit children with physical and mental disabilities (11).

Specialized institutions and residential schools emerged with varying ideas about the people who lived in them and their needs. In the United States, there came to be more and more institutions organized around a particular type of disability. Within institutions, a number of notions shaped goals and practices. The most significant for disabled people was the increasing influence of medical personnel and practices. Although medicine didn't overtly claim expertise in reducing the economic liability posed by disabled people, it did corner the market on attempts to contain the perceived negative social impact of disability. This is most clearly seen in the growing influence of medicine on the response to mental illness and the shift from the mid-nineteenth century to the early twentieth century from custodial care of people with mental illnesses to belief in the efficacy of prevention and cure. Although superintendents of custodial institutions often had medical training, their work came to be seen as policing and restraining people. The medical establishment launched attacks on asylums, asserting their practice was unscientific because they were offering custodial care with no proven ability to treat or cure.

Adolf Meyer led the "mental hygiene" movement, a program that elevated the role of psychiatrists in not only treatment but prevention. The institutions that emerged in the twentieth century became teaching hospitals and research centers. Along with this trend in institutional care, spurred by a new orientation to scientific progress, came a belief in aftercare, which "looked not to the chronic, but to the curable patient, not to custody but to adjustment, not to continued dependence but to independence" (Rothman 1980, 313). The practices were reminiscent of the way some communities had responded to mental illness before the growth of institutions.

Of course, had this push toward independence and productivity for people with mental illness and other disabilities been successful, and had the government assured the type of support and equality of opportunity that would have allowed disabled people to live in

49

the community, the history of disabled people in the twentieth century would look much different than it does. Some of the innovative medical interventions and growing expertise might then have been coupled with a commitment to independent living, active participation in the community, and, possibly, with concern for rights and equality. Instead, institutionalization and medical control became the norm for many disabled people.

The idea that disabled people are, in an absolute sense, an economic and social liability is rarely challenged. The belief that disabled people impede progress or increase the vulnerability of a society, particularly when it is under siege, has never been tested, and certainly has never been tested in a society that works to maximize the productivity and participation of disabled people. The financial stability of society does not seem to be the factor that determines greater degrees of acceptance and participation. Indeed, Hanks and Hanks (1948) conclude their discussion of this category by commenting that economic considerations alone don't determine response to disability. They remind us that although some of the groups they discuss resort to infanticide or other means of eliminating disabled people when there are scant resources, "the Paiute of the Great Basin of North America, who had an almost equally precarious margin of existence, neither practiced infanticide nor abandoned their disabled. . . ." And the Australians, who "had a slim margin of surplus" did practice infanticide but "seem not to have disposed of the physically handicapped" (16).

In the current climate in the United States of managed health care, there is a deep fear among disabled people that our lives will be weighed on an economic scale. In Michael Bérubé's (1996) book about his family's experience of having a child born with Down syndrome, he speaks poignantly of that fear:

Among the many things I fear coming to pass in my children's lifetime, I fear this above all: that children like James will eventually be seen as "luxuries" employers and insurance companies cannot afford, or as "luxuries" the nation or the planet cannot afford. I do not want to see a world in which human life is judged by the kind of cost-benefit analysis that weeds out those least likely to attain self-sufficiency and to provide adequate "returns" on social investments. (52)

3. TOLERANT UTILIZATION

One can infer from the examples provided under the Hankses' (1948) category Tolerant Utilization that they recognized situations in which disabled people, although often marginal figures in the society, are allowed to participate to the extent that they have the ability to fulfill certain roles and duties designated by the nondisabled majority as necessary. Disabled people's actions therefore are at the will and bidding of the nondisabled majority. For instance, during World War II disabled people worked in record numbers because so many "able-bodied" people were at war. During this time women (both disabled and nondisabled) were also employed in positions never before open to them. At the close of the war, these groups returned to their previously low levels of employment and to the restricted range of positions they were allowed to occupy.

Another example of disabled people being utilized as needed by the society are situations in which they are considered more useful or practical in certain roles than nondisabled people. For instance, the utilization of hearing-impaired and deaf workers on assembly lines where noisy machinery is used or of people of short stature in tight spaces where larger workers cannot fit. Although gainful employment is always desirable in a drastically underemployed group and there is a certain peculiar logic to these solutions, given the economic vulnerability and low social status of men and women with disabilities, these situations are ripe for exploitation. Further, the particular health and safety issues for these workers and the lack of control or free will in such situations make them highly dubious opportunities.

Disabled people have also served at the dominant culture's pleasure as fools and jesters in a royal court, and in such social institutions and rituals as freak shows and carnivals. People have been put on public display in circuses and other more sedate institutions, such as museums and medical facilities. (Bogdan 1988, 1996; Thomson 1996). A man described as the "Elephant Man" and a woman called the "Hottentot Venus" were put on view in medical and scientific settings, as well as in commercial venues. People have worked in these areas out of economic necessity or because they were under the "care" of medical personnel and had little opportunity to pursue other goals. Either as scientific specimens or amusements displayed for profit, people with disabilities were denied basic rights and freedoms. Although the large buttocks and genitalia of the "Hottentot Venus" are not disabilities by most current legal and typical definitions, her body and that of the "Elephant Man" were considered pathological by social standards.

A final example boldly illuminates the utilitarian and exploitive nature of some people's ideas about disabled women and men, and about women in general:

> When geneticist Sharlene George was interviewed for admission into a graduate program at Stanford University in 1967, the department chair said: "Miss George, do you know why I'm interviewing you? It's because this year I'm reduced to the lame, the halt, the blind, and the women." (Todd 1984, 44)

The next three categories, Limited Participation, Laissez-Faire, and Participation and Accommodation, are presented together and then used to discuss the continuum in educational practice in the United States from the seventeenth century to the present.

4. LIMITED PARTICIPATION

The category Limited Participation is the least specific in the Hankses' typology and the examples provided are the most ambiguous, yet I find the term useful to describe situations in which disabled people's roles and status are largely derived from their ability to be productive in terms of the standards set by the dominant majority. This idea is based on an individual model of disability, the idea that it is up to the individual to demonstrate worth and competence. It promotes a false sense of acceptance because the norms and standards of the able-bodied majority are imposed and held up as the ideal to which all should aspire. Whereas the previous category, Tolerant Utilization, speaks to the society's control not only of criteria for performance but of domains in which competence can be demonstrated, Limited Participation indicates the society's willingness to accept a disabled person among its ranks in any domain in which she or he can "keep up" with the nondisabled.

5. LAISSEZ-FAIRE

In the Hankses' (1948) description of their last category, Laissez-Faire, "a steadfast relation to the protective group, despite handicap," is observed and "the obligation of the extended family to shelter and provide for its unfortunates continues, whether they are able to give their labor or not" (18–19). I've eliminated the terms "protective group" and "provide for its unfortunates," two ideas that do not capture the more complex relations that occur among disabled and nondisabled people, and propose instead that the category include situations in which relations between nondisabled and disabled people exist, and where the family and community provide varying degrees of support for disabled people, whether they are able to work or not. Although in such situations the society does not overtly exclude disabled people, it does not work toward accommodation, social justice, and equity with respect to them.

I am proposing that the idea of noninterference implied by the term *laissez-faire* applies to the social structures and not to specific responses to disabled people. Indeed, in such situations there may be various types of concern displayed for disabled people and interventions provided, yet if the norms of the able-bodied majority are centered and held up as the ultimate goal of all people, and the society makes no effort to reconstruct its goals or acceptable means of achieving them to reflect a broader range of citizens, the society has adopted a laissez-faire approach to disability. In such situations, the dominant group decides what disabled people need and attempts to meet those needs but does little to engage with disabled people as a constituency to work together to set the terms of accommodation. Disabled people then are left in the unenviable position of having to keep up with norms and standards but with no opportunity to shape them.

6. PARTICIPATION AND ACCOMMODATION

I've added the last category, Participation and Accommodation, to the Hankses' typology in order to report on the moments and places in which a proactive stance is evident toward the equitable participation of all members of the society. These are admittedly rare events, but there are some examples of concerted efforts to accommodate all members of the group and to adapt the procedures and standards typically imposed to reflect a range of abilities, interests, and needs. This does not mean lowering standards in an absolute sense; it means that greater flexibility is evident and a broader range of objectives are set. These actions are based on moral, practical, religious, and/or rights-based approaches to full participation of all members of society.

Throughout the history of the United States, education for disabled children has assumed many forms, from complete denial of formalized instruction to a few recent examples of exciting, well-informed, and inclusive classrooms where disabled and nondisabled children learn together in cooperative groups designed to maximize the participation of all children in the learning process. Between these extremes, disabled children have experienced a variety of learning environments.

There are segregated settings, including classrooms in institutions; specialized residential and day schools, designed either for children with specific disabilities or for mixed disability groupings; and separate special education classrooms within a general education school. A variety of other types of placements for disabled children have emerged since the 1975 passage of PL94–142, "which guaranteed an education for the nation's eight million children with disabilities . . . in the least restrictive environment, that is with nondisabled children whenever possible" (Shapiro 1993, 166). These options include the common practice of placing some children who are identified as "special education" students in a general education class for one or two periods a day, or, for a few children, in the those classrooms for whole day, if they can keep up with the academic curriculum. This practice of incorporating students in general education for part or all of the day is generally known as "mainstreaming," even though that is not a legal term. The total integration of all disabled children in general education is known as "inclusion" and exists currently in a number of isolated schools and in a few school districts around the country. In inclusive schools all children attend their neighborhood school, and are placed in classes based on age rather than on test results, evaluation, diagnosis, or past performance. Although inclusion is a very recent project of schools, there has not been a straightforward historical march from complete denial of education for those considered outcasts or pariahs through to totally inclusive and integrated classrooms.

The education system throughout the history of the United States exemplifies the range of responses demonstrated in the six categories presented in this chapter. The three categories just presented, Limited Participation, Laissez-Faire, and Participation and Accommodation, are particularly useful in distinguishing among the recent approaches to educating disabled children. Although the connections between the Hankses' typology and the educational practices described here are somewhat forced, I will describe how the ideology underlying each of their categories might lead to particular educational practices. When disabled people are considered pariahs, education, if provided at all, is aimed at containment and control. It might also have a taming function: to civilize creatures seen as not quite human. Any of the general goals of education—intellectual development, acculturation, employment, or preparation for participation in the democracy—would not be considered useful or worthwhile for people thought to be a threat to society, or incapable or unworthy of citizenship. However, to the extent that education is thought to decrease the dangerous, unwanted characteristics of disabled people, then it would be conducted in a situation isolated from others, with goals of social control and order imposed rather than individual enhancement. These agendas were more obvious in institutions and asylums of the past, but I am not convinced that the ideology has disappeared. At any given moment, whether in an institution of the eighteenth or twentieth century, or a general education school today, the idea that disabled people are to be controlled can influence a number of different types of educational initiatives.

When education is guided by the idea that disabled people are Economic and Social Liabilities, then instruction will be geared toward decreasing the drain. Indeed, any educational intervention, short of the most proactive, rights-based approach to the education of all children, can be seen as responding to a need to reduce the economic and social burden disabled people are thought to represent. Rather than see the mission of education of disabled children in terms of intellectual and social development, preparing them to partake in the rights and pleasures of citizenship, the orientation that guides this approach is more focused on vocational training and on the tools and skills needed to become productive and self-sufficient. Similar interpretations have been made along class and race lines of the imperatives that drive education.

These liability themes emerge in debates over what is the most cost-efficient means of educating disabled students. When moral and pedagogically based arguments for inclusive education are presented, they are often countered by economic arguments presented at school board meetings or in legislative bodies about the drain that educating disabled children is on community resources. However, the concerns raised about allocating resources to disabled children's education are based on local and immediate economic analyses. Broader, long-term analyses are often not part of these discussions, thereby bypassing recognition of the long-term consequences of denying children equitable education and the long-term gains that could be realized from an educated and prepared cadre of disabled children. In addition to the economic liability themes, concerns are also raised about whether the presence of disabled children in a general education classroom deflects attention from the needs of the nondisabled children. Each of these is a practical problem but also an ethical problem. My purpose here is to uncover the ethos that drives the decisions.

The values that underlie the Tolerant Utilization approach may subtly influence a school toward preparing disabled people to fulfill the functions that the nondisabled majority are in need of. Recall that in this category are the situations in which disabled people, though treated as marginal figures in the society, are incorporated as needed if they have the ability to fulfill certain roles and duties designated by the nondisabled majority as useful. Therefore, pedagogy and curriculum are not guided by a concern for equality of opportunity but, rather, a utilitarian vision of educating disabled people. Special education classrooms, institutional settings, and sheltered workshops whose curriculum is influenced by this restricted and stereotyped vision of appropriate roles of disabled people qualify as examples in this category.

The categories Limited Participation and Laissez-Faire apply to situations in which standards for disabled people's performance are set by the dominant majority, and it is up to the individual to demonstrate worth and competence in terms of these criteria. This description could apply to schools that have mainstreaming programs for some disabled children and separate special education classes for others. Children with physical disabilities or sensory impairments may be mainstreamed for a few or all periods a day in general education classes if they can keep up with the academic level of the class. In settings such as these you often see students popped in and out of classrooms, put into a general education reading class if they show skill in this area but returned to the special education classroom or to a resource room if their skill is not considered equivalent to the general education students.

Some schools with mainstreaming programs have created wonderful, innovative programs to incorporate some of the disabled children into their general education classes. These programs provide more systematic interactions between nondisabled and disabled children, and the school provides support for some disabled children in more integrated classroom environments, even if the disabled children are not able to engage in or complete all the same tasks that nondisabled children can. Disabled children are eligible for such programs if they can keep up in most academic areas with the children identified as nondisabled. If they are not able to meet those requirements, segregated specialized education is provided, designed on a priori decisions made about their academic and social capabilities. Although the class or the school does not overtly exclude disabled people, it does not work toward full accommodation or equity with respect to disabled children.

In situations such as these, the basic structure of schools and classrooms remains unchanged, but some disabled children are shifted into general education as long as they can keep up and their presence results in minimal alteration of the prevailing structure. The children's welfare may be of great concern to the school and the community, yet the vision of what can or should be done to create a more equitable environment is limited.

My objective here is not to indict the much-maligned special education teachers or programs. There is probably as broad a range of quality of education in general as in special education. The point is that mainstreaming and other moderate solutions are token programs that cull from the special education rosters the children who are most like the "mainstream." The system places them in classrooms where their presence is contingent on their behaving as much like the nondisabled children as possible. If drooling or having spasms or a speech impairment is not within the school's or the district's criteria for acceptable behaviors for mainstreamed classrooms, the child will be locked out of general education. This places the mainstreamed children in the awkward position of having to look and act as nondisabled as possible to maintain their position in general education and, as a result, it marginalizes even more the disabled children who can never play those parts. Further, and rarely discussed, mainstreamed children lose the opportunity to be with other disabled children. Mainstreaming doesn't erase the line between disabled and nondisabled people; it just draws the line between acceptable and not acceptable a little to the left or, if you're sitting on the opposite side, to the right.

For the past ten years in particular, the practices in most school districts have hovered between those whose overt structure resembles the Limited Participation and Laissez-Faire models. The other ideas, that disabled people are pariahs, social and economic burdens, and people to be utilized in society if and when they are needed, filters through educational discourse in more covert and intangible ways.

Recall that the distinguishing features of the last category, Accommodation and Participation, are that a proactive stance is taken toward equitable participation, and where procedures and standards are adapted to include everyone. The newest model of education, full inclusion, is the closest to such an accommodating environment. It differs from all the categories above in that in its most thorough and successful forms, all children go to their neighborhood school and all are incorporated in general education classes with appropriate supports and accommodations. The pedagogical practices and curriculum are designed to reach a broad range of children, and integration and active participation are goals the school is committed to. Whereas the practice of mainstreaming has been restricted primarily to children with physical disabilities and sensory impairments, the inclusion model incorporates all children, whatever their disability, in a general education classroom. Therefore, children with mental retardation, autism, or mental illnesses, those who are typically the most sequestered of all children, participate in the learning and social activities of inclusive classrooms. This is a startling idea for many people, particularly if they have never seen it in action. In classroom environments such as these, the criteria for demonstrating competence may not be the same for all children, but together the group tackles the subject matter and each child engages with it in a manner consistent with her or his aptitudes and needs. Goals and standards are shifted not downward but out, to a more flexible and broader means of demonstrating competence. The burden to "keep up" is shifted off the individual student, and the whole classroom environment shifts in its overall procedures and expectations to maximize learning for all.

The report of the National Center on Educational Restructuring and Inclusion (1995) on the status of inclusive education in the United States provides qualitative data on the benefits and problems in the transformation of schools to inclusive sites. Multiple examples underscore the positive transformations in the behavior and learning patterns of disabled students who have been transferred from special education classrooms to inclusive ones. Students who had previously required a great deal of adult intervention to sit still, to be quiet, to focus on lessons and not distract other students appear to respond to peer pressure to behave, and teachers are reported to spend much more time on instruction than on "parenting" behaviors such as "setting and enforcing guidelines of appropriate behavior" (226). An example from Burbank, California, describes one way that a school accommodated children who are deaf. The school draws children who are deaf from a wide area and, as a result, from one-third to two-thirds of the students in any given class are deaf. The regular school curriculum is maintained by using a team-teaching approach (one general education teacher and one teacher trained in special education, both fluent in sign language). All students participate in the same classes and recreational activities, with a high degree of social interaction among deaf and hearing students. The district report indicates that "there is no isolation of the deaf students, in the classroom or playground. Hearing students sign . . . and at the eighth-grade graduation ceremony, the three hearing students who were chosen as speakers (the fourth was deaf) each signed their speech" (39).

Inclusion is not an educational plan to benefit disabled children. It is a model for educating all children equitably. The concept of heterogeneous grouping is supported by data from studies of detracking,[2] which indicate that the benefits of detracking accrue to all children. The benefits for the nondisabled children are not solely that they learn tolerance and acceptance. Although I don't want to minimize the importance of that lesson, the benefits are broader than the moral lessons such exposure can offer. For instance, when nondeaf children learn sign language, they are not only exposed to a second language, rare these days in most elementary schools but come to understand something about language itself and how it functions in human experience. The presence, let's say, of children with mental retardation in a classroom not only helps the children who have never had such exposure see the disabled children as complex human beings, recognize their strengths and weaknesses, and learn from their abilities but teach all the children how to interact to solve problems and about the range of ways that people approach a task. The children who learn more slowly can pick up cues from children who have mastered a particular domain, and the children who have mastered it can benefit from explaining it, paraphrasing and highlighting important points, and also, significantly, can benefit from watching the steps that the learners go through in mastering the material. A range of types of learners in the classroom provides teachers with many "teachable moments," the occasions when the spontaneous curriculum that arises in classroom interactions enriches learning.

I want to resist the impulse to overromanticize inclusive education. These described benefits don't always get realized. Inclusion has not been an unmitigated success wherever it has been implemented. Insufficient teacher preparation, overcrowding, and understaffing can interfere with the best of plans. Further, this plan for integrated environments in schools is taking place in a society that is far from integrated. Neither the children nor the teachers and parents have much experience with integrated communities. There have been instances where disabled children have been disruptive, where nondisabled children have rejected disabled children and they remain isolated in the classroom, and where teachers are overwhelmed and underprepared, and resent teaching in this type of heterogeneously grouped classroom. Those problems may always occur, although there are certainly ways to decrease them.

Although integration is a goal of the disability rights community in education and in society as a whole, it does not stem from a valorization of the nondisabled, nor should it be read solely as a reaction to the quality of special education. "Normalization" is a spurious goal and not a useful way to think about the push to inclusive education. Herbert Kohl (1994) makes a similar point about the misinterpretation of the *Brown vs. Board of Education* decision when he notes that "the specific wording of the decision— 'Separate education facilities are inherently unequal'—has racist implications," and he then distinguishes between involuntary and voluntary segregation (92). He reports on the high quality of teaching that occurred in many all-black schools.

What is wrong with special education, then, is not that the quality of instruction is necessarily inferior or that there are only disabled children in the classrooms. What is problematic is that these are often isolated, stigmatized classes, and that placement in special education is not voluntary. Segregated special education is bedeviled by the stigma that all members of the school, whether consciously or not, attach to the designation. All the children in the school, the staff, and parents know which classes are special education classes. No matter what kinds of overt lessons are taught at the school about respect for difference or other such seemingly committed agendas with weak impact, the hidden curriculum, the stronger message, is that children in special education are different, incompetent and unsavory, and, because of their isolation, easily avoidable. Expectations that the school, the disabled and nondisabled children, the parents, and the teachers have are inevitably lowered by these designations. Most damaging of all, the negative expectations are assimilated and internalized by the disabled children with devastating long-term consequences.

Segregated education is not inherently worse than integrated education because it is inhabited by disabled children. It is functionally worse because it is a restricted environment, with classes so small that the benefits of individualized instruction are often overshadowed by the limited types of interactions children can have with one another, and often by the dominance of adults who may interfere with children's opportunities to learn from and with one another. Children in special education may learn a great deal. Indeed, there have been wonderful special education classes with dedicated and knowledgeable teachers, but as Jeffrey Libby, an integration-support teacher for an inclusive elementary school, points out, "One of the biggest arguments against inclusion . . . is that disabled students can acquire more skills within an isolated setting . . . but you teach things in isolation, and they're only good in isolation" (Casanave 1991, 41).

Although integration is sought for the breadth of educational opportunities offered and other advantages, dismantling special education will, unfortunately, diminish disabled children's opportunities to grow and learn around other children with disabilities, which gives them the opportunity to shape this essential part of their identity in the company of others who share their experience. Children with disabilities are hungry for role models, and other children may be the only disabled people in a child's life. Exposure to other disabled children's adaptiveness, understanding of their social position, sense of self, ability to negotiate in the world, and basic information make these friendships critical in development. In an inclusive setting there may be only one or two children with disabilities in a classroom.

School districts that support inclusion are among the most consciously rendered participatory and accommodating environments known, yet there have been other moments and places in the world where integration has been spotted. For the most part these have been more spontaneous, chance events rather than purposefully constructed environments, and the accommodations are usually not for all disabled people, just groups who achieve certain significance in the culture. It is critical that these be noted. They speak to the human capacity to construct disability very differently than it usually is.

One of the most thoroughly investigated environments is described in a landmark study conducted by Nora Groce (1985) and reported in her book *Everyone Here Spoke Sign Language*. It is an ethnohistory of Martha's Vineyard, where, for more than two centuries ending in the 1950s, a high incidence of hereditary deafness existed. Rather than focus on the condition itself, Groce focuses on the accommodations that some communities on the island made to this subgroup of their population. The deaf and hearing residents lived and worked together as equals, and, as the book's title suggests, most people on the Vineyard were fluent in a signed language that evolved there. It should be noted that although the proportion of deaf residents was larger than usual, in the course of the three centuries in which this hereditary phenomenon occurred only about 72 people with hereditary deafness lived on the island, one in every 155 people; the typical ratio in the United States in the nineteenth century was one in every 5,728 people. Therefore, the deaf on the island were significantly more proportionately, but the use of sign language by the whole community was in response to a rather small absolute number.

In interviews with members of the community who could remember the time when the deaf residents were still around, what comes across most vividly is the matter-of-fact way that they spoke of their deaf neighbors, and of their own accommodation to their presence. Groce (1985) notes that "the community's attitude can be judged also from the fact that until I asked a direct question on the subject, most of my informants never even considered anything unusual about the manner in which their deaf townsmen were integrated into the society" (51). But a reporter for the *Boston Sunday Herald* knew there was something unusual occurring there. Groce quotes an 1895 story:

> The kindly and well-informed people whom I saw, strange to say, seem to be proud of the affliction—to regard it as a kind of plume in the hat of the stock. Elsewhere the afflicted are screened as much as possible from public notoriety. But these people gave

me a great lot of photographs, extending back four generations. These pictures of people who have never spoken a word from the day of their birth, create the impression of the invasion by deafness of what might otherwise have been a wonderfully perfect type.

The reporter presaged the deaf pride movement by almost one hundred years and displayed some understanding of the social construction of disability. However, the ableist notion that the deaf people would be perfect if not for their impairments and a later comment that "the mutes are not uncomfortable in their deprivation" (52–53) reveal the limitations of the reporter's insight.

How would a reporter today approach a story on a similar but more circumscribed environment, for instance, the Burbank, California, school, discussed earlier, where hearing and nonhearing students learn and play together and where both groups are fluent in sign language? Would she or he frame the subjects as less than perfect, albeit valiant and plucky, and the hearing kids as generous and good-spirited? Paint the relationships between the two groups in sentimentalized colors? Glorify the accomplishments of the deaf children? Or might a reporter today have the sophistication and insight about disability issues to focus on how an accommodating environment structures equality and motivates both groups to work together utilizing a range of communications media that allows full participation of everyone? Even if a reporter did have that sophistication and insight, she or he would have to contend with the overwhelming tendency of most news stories today to go for the uplifting human interest story rather than an analysis of the structural elements that determine interpersonal relationships. This is true of the media in general, but in the case of disability, the likelihood is magnified a thousand times.

Representations of disability and the representations of disabled people's place in society are largely in the hands of people schooled in a particular vision of disability, one that is saturated with deterministic thinking and characterized by maudlin and morbid sentiments projected onto disabled people's experience. The insistence not just that disability is an unfortunate occurrence but that disabled people are, perforce, "unfortunates" seeps into most reports on the disability experience. Insiders' reports of disability, as seen in some of the best of the disability studies scholarship and in such publications as the *Disability Rag* and the *Mouth*, present a different perspective.

The Martha's Vineyard study also stands in contrast to typical records of disabled people in society because it documents a Participatory and Accommodating environment, focuses on social determinants, and is comprehensive. The dearth of such reports raises a number of questions that I address below. Have there been no other such environments? Does the absence in history of similar environments indicate the impossibility of such integration and equity? Are researchers not interested in such social patterns? Do researchers lack the theoretical tools with which to evaluate such behaviors and practices?

I believe there have been and are places and moments where more equitable and integrated environments are seen. They are not ideal; indeed, Martha's Vineyard is far from ideal because the accommodation made to deaf people did not extend to all disabled people. These are places where the nondisabled center and dominance shifts and greater degrees of accommodation are evident. John Hockenberry (1995) describes the neighborhood around Israel's most famous acute trauma facility, at Tel Hashomer Hospital, where most people who were wounded in the wars or in automobile accidents go for rehabilitation. It seems the disabled men (it is not clear where disabled women go) stay on in the neighborhood after they leave the hospital, and Hockenberry, a reporter for National Public Radio and a wheelchair user, noted a concentration of houses with "newly built wide doors, ramped entrances, and freshly paved driveways," quite different from most Israeli neighborhoods. The area, though, was "something of a crip ghetto, the only place in Israel where I would regularly see people in wheelchairs on the street" (236).

Anyone who has ever visited a well-run independent living center[3] would witness an environment consciously rendered to accommodate all people. In addition to the offices themselves, in the immediate neighborhood of these centers, you are more likely to see ramps to get into stores, accessible bathrooms in local restaurants, and possibly menus in Braille. In some instances, the independent living center has had a strong impact on local policy.

Berkeley, California was the site of the first independent living center in the country (incorporated in 1972), and is notable for its history of strong activism and high degree of local impact. Anyone with an interest in such phenomena would notice the curb cuts on every corner and the ramps into buildings. When I first visited Berkeley in 1975, what was even more striking to me was the degree to which disability had become such a common feature of the landscape that I could move about casually without causing a stir. People, it appeared to me, did not stare nor did they glance and quickly avert their eyes. People were, in general, neither rude nor overly solicitous. The shifts that had occurred in the physical and communications environments, and the strong presence of an active disability community have these kinds of effects on the interpersonal environment.

Granted, there are very few places like independent living centers and their environs where disabled people have much autonomy and freedom of movement. Only a few other examples come to mind. One is some of the newly designed areas in the National Parks System, where disabled people and nondisabled people have worked together to make the environments accessible. Another is a small, rustic resort I visited in Byron Bay, Australia, run by disabled people in a place where pleasure and good times are the order of the day. Other places include meetings of disability rights groups or disability studies conferences.

These places are remarkable for disabled people. They differ from most of the places encountered, in which inequities, discrimination, and marginalization are more likely to occur. These places are so radically different from typical experience and yet so clearly possible that they remind us of the absence of will to create such environments everywhere. Thinking about this situation brings to mind a study reported in the *New York Times* Science section a few years ago. The article (Wilford, 1994) reviewed the results of a two-year investigation by an anthropologist of the sparsely populated island of Vanatinai near Papua New Guinea. Its front-page headline read "Sexes Equal on South Sea Isle." Dr. Maria Lepowsky reported that a unique social arrangement exists: men and women live and work as virtual equals. "It is not a place where men and women live in perfect harmony and where the privileges and burdens of both sexes are exactly equal, but it comes close" (C1). She said that the findings challenge some theorists' position that male dominance is universal or somehow inherent in human cultures.

The value and meaning of Lepowsky's discovery was, I think, apparent to most *Times* readers. Vanatinai differs from other known cultures around the world in its apparently high degree of gender equity. Would the readers have a similarly sophisticated understanding of, let's say, the meaning and significance of the anthropological data collected on Martha's Vineyard? Are they ready to consider that the social position of disabled people in the United States and in most other known cultures is not inevitable and immutable. It took the tools of women's studies to uncover the key ingredients of the Vanatinai culture. Similarly, disability studies is needed to investigate equitable arrangements and apply that knowledge to the construction of equitable societies. Until disability studies articulated the social and political paradigms, there was little in the way of a theoretical framework from which such research could proceed.

The title of this chapter, "Divided Society," speaks to the fissures between disabled and nondisabled people evident across time and across cultures. I contend these divides are not inevitable; indeed, if we mobilize sufficient intellectual wherewithal, I believe we can unearth other positive arrangements or, at least, envision what they might look like. In the next chapter I turn to the academy to investigate its role in marginalizing the knowledge and the people needed to reposition disabled people in the social and political arena.

NOTES

1. See also Eiesland's (1994) *The Disabled God: Toward a Liberatory Theology of Disability* for an overview of religious explanations of disability.
2. For discussions of tracking and detracking, see McLaren (1994); Oakes (1985); and Polakow (1993).
3. Independent living centers are organizations run by and for disabled people, operating on the premise that, as Joseph Shapiro (1993) writes in *No Pity*, no one "knew more about the needs of disabled people than disabled people themselves" (73). The centers provide services that allow people with disabilities to achieve maximum independence in the community and at the same time serve as advocates to change the community to make it more accessible and equitable for disabled people.

4

DIVIDED CURRICULUM

The gates of the institutions and sheltered dwellings that have housed disabled people over the centuries have been opened. The critical gaze of our newly minted citizens, unaccounted for all these years, is now trained on the dominant narratives. Through their eyes, we see the replication and justification of social practices in our intellectual traditions. This chapter provides a disability reading of those traditions, as well as a discussion of the obstacles to meaningful inquiry.

Butler and Walters (1991) note that decisions about curriculum transformation are based, in part, on the answer to the question "Are these ignored, distorted, subordinated people and their histories and legacies, and experiences important to understanding and expressing our American selves?" (326). To get the academy to engage that question with respect to disability, disability rights activists and disability studies scholars have first had to assume the responsibility of proving that disabled people occupy a subordinate position in critical social and economic domains, that disabled people are a significant constituency, and that our histories and legacies have been distorted. Further, disability studies has demonstrated how the status and assigned roles of disabled people are not inevitable outcomes of impairments but the products of social and political processes. Now it is incumbent on people across the disciplines to study the consequences of oppressing people with disabilities and, significantly, to study the consequences of constructing a knowledge base within which that social positioning is deemed rational and morally sound.

In directing attention now to the role of the academy in the social response to disability, I will focus on three domains. The first is the nature of inquiry into disability; the second, the structure of the curriculum in higher education and its role in organizing information so as to represent certain versions of the world; and the third, the content of the curriculum.

1. INQUIRY

Research, whether aimed at disability as subject matter and disabled people as subjects or erroneously ignoring disability, plays a role in constructing disability. A number of questions arise when thinking about how the method and focus of the process of acquiring new knowledge shape understanding of disability. For instance, how does the structure and focus of research contribute to ableist notions of disability? What perspectives inform the choice of variables, theories to be tested, interpretative frameworks to be employed, and subjects/objects to be studied? How has the research agenda been influenced by the absence of disabled people in academic positions?

I will start with the last question. Disabled people are rarely in the researcher's position because of a host of factors, including limited educational opportunities, discrimination in hiring and promotion, and inadequate support for disability studies scholarship. Further, when disabled people have attained academic positions, the types of accommodations that would facilitate active research production are often not provided. For instance, material available in Braille or on tape, sign language interpreters, readers, work stations in the library or in labs that people who use wheelchairs can access, or other low- or high-tech equipment, such as voice-activated computers. As a result of discrimination in hiring and in providing access to the materials and facilities needed to engage in research, one seldom finds in one person the expertise of the trained researcher combined with the expertise of the disabled subject.

Typically, disabled people are studied only in their particularity, which is not considered generalizable or relevant to nondisabled people, or they are studied as deviation from the norm in order to increase the knowledge about and stature of the norm. In social science and science research, where the vast majority of research has been conducted, there is the body of research that focuses on disability to learn about that experience, and then research designed to learn about standard functioning by measuring deficits and anomalies in disabled people. Other research renders disabled people invisible and irrelevant as an object of inquiry. For instance, research that purports to represent a particular population is likely to cull its sample from nondisabled people, yet the description of the limitations of generalizability of the data rarely acknowledges this omission.

Tavris (1992) in *The Mismeasure of Woman* describes a similar phenomenon with respect to gender. A review of medical journals found that titles of articles that implied a general population, such as "Normal Human Aging," were frequently used for studies with only male subjects. In contrast, the titles of articles reporting research exclusively on women, stated that fact explicitly. Stephen Jay Gould (1981) acknowledges this tendency with respect to both gender and race, and explains that the title of his book, *Mismeasure of Man*, is intended to comment on the tendency of scientists to "study 'man' (that is, white European males), regarding this group as a standard and everybody else as something to be measured unfavorably against it" (16).

In addition to the marginalization of disabled people as objects of inquiry and the failure to see connections among disabled and nondisabled people's experience, the relationship between disability and its "owner" has not been adequately studied. This is a relationship that could be studied throughout the curriculum, using the lenses of literary criticism, philosophy, history, poetry, anthropology, women's studies, and numerous other perspectives. The majority of research has occurred in the sciences and social sciences, particularly psychology, but that research has not yielded very rich, contextualized knowledge. It is not clear to me, though, whether the quality of the data is a result of prevailing research methods or whether the choice of methodology is determined by prevailing ideas about disability. For instance, have empiricism's reductive tendencies forced us to examine impairments and functional limitations over the more complex and nuanced experience that disabled people describe as the texture of their lives? Or have ideas about disability, such as deterministic beliefs, the medicalization of disability, or the objectification of disabled people, led researchers to employ quantitative rather than qualitative, historical, or interpretive methods?

Both quantitative and qualitative methods have been used predominantly to study individual patterns, not social situations or cultural representations that influence those patterns. Even if these methods were employed to focus on the powerful—those who exercise control over disabled people—and were employed by disabled people to do so, they would not adequately assess the process of ableism. Oliver (1992), and Ward and Flynn (1994) call for an emancipatory paradigm that, as Oliver says, "stems from the gradual rejection of the positivist view of social research as the pursuit of absolute knowledge through the scientific method and the gradual disillusionment with the interpretive view of such research as the generation of socially useful knowledge within particular historical and social contexts." He proposes that the emancipatory model involve "recognition of and confrontation with power which structures the social relations of research production" (110).

Although it seems that recent interest in qualitative methods could improve the study of disability, several scholars have challenged this assumption. Oliver (1992) faults both positivism and interpretive paradigms for their contribution to the alienation of the researcher from the researched, whereas Rioux and Bach (1994) point to the more general "positivist theory of knowledge" as the root cause of the reification of disability (viii). Ward and Flynn (1994) describe how both traditional positivist research paradigms and interpretive or qualitative paradigms can be used by "relatively powerful *experts* on relatively powerless 'subjects.'" They go on to say that "despite the liberal trappings of the qualitative paradigm, the 'social relations of research production' had not changed" (30–31). In other words, these newer methods have not succeeded in placing disabled people in a more central role in research production, nor in explicating the power differences between predominantly nondisabled researchers and their disabled "subjects."

Gould (1981) raises similar questions about methodology in relation to racism. He asks, "[Did] the introduction of inductive science add legitimate data to change or strengthen a nascent argument for racial ranking? Or did a priori commitment to ranking fashion the 'scientific questions asked and even the data gathered to support a foreordained conclusion'?" (31). The questions have as much to do with disability as they do with racism. The process of ranking and the spurious constructs within which the ranked are grouped need to be examined not only in terms of the disproportionate numbers of African Americans who have received a low rank but in terms of the fabrication of such a system and the legitimization of ranking.

I am reminded of this faulty logic when I read exposes of the disproportionate representation of black males in special education. I view that overrepresentation as a moral failure, and as a destructive and aggressive act. Yet I am simultaneously disturbed that the placement of any child in isolated and restrictive educational settings is not also challenged. The pathological designations and labels affixed to disabled girls and boys carry tremendous weight and determine a vast range of experience. The medicalized classification system and the use of diagnostic categories legitimize ranking in the education system, and there has been inadequate attention to the social determinants of these categories. The history of their construction and use demonstrates how the knowledge of the medical profession has been privileged and is used to maintain the social position of the diagnosed.

2. STRUCTURE OF CURRICULUM

The dominant questions related to the structure of the curriculum are, How are domains of knowledge divided up or clustered so as to render a partial or distorted picture of disability? How does this configuration lead to particular social practices?

The disciplinary and divisional structure can be thought of as a medium by which content is delivered. Although not a technological device per se, it shapes and molds the contained ideas, forcing certain connections while obscuring others. Disability studies scholarship calls into question the utility and validity of the present configuration, and the consequences of these divisions on the content of the curriculum.

THE DIVIDE BETWEEN THE LIBERAL ARTS AND THE APPLIED FIELDS

A major dividing line that stretches the entire length of the curriculum is that between the applied fields and the liberal arts. Although there is variation across the country in where different fields are maintained, a department's or division's identity is shaped by whether it is predominantly devoted to teaching the liberal arts or preparing students for the helping professions. Courses in each domain, even if they are similar, rarely traverse the divide, nor do faculty. For instance, a course in child development in a teacher education program is often not interchangeable with the same-titled course in the psychology department, even though both might be taught by faculty trained in the same area. Another example is that American Sign Language (ASL) is more likely to be taught in the applied programs as a tool to communicate with Deaf clients or students than taught as a language and cultural heritage in a liberal arts framework. Although there have been some changes in recent years, students are rarely allowed to use ASL to fulfill language requirements on the graduate or undergraduate level, no matter their level of proficiency.

The liberal arts and applied fields achieve different status in the academy, derived in no small measure from ideas about the supposed theory-driven nature of liberal arts and the more pragmatic imperatives of the applied fields. The theory-based domains are thought to demand a greater degree of abstract reasoning; the applied fields are believed to require the more concrete thinking skills of a practitioner. In reviewing the history of the dichotomy, Minnich (1990) notes that "the liberal arts were for those who could indulge in study of the 'higher' things; the servile arts, for those whose knowledge would be put to some direct use. The old privileged-male Athenian notion remained—the idea that which is of no use (that is, is an end in itself) is higher than anything that is involved intimately with the maintenance of life" (45). All focused study of disability occurs in those applied fields which are designed to prepare practitioners to work in education or health care institutions with disabled people.

Knowledge generated within the liberal arts is, of course, often applied to social problems. "Many of the social sciences developed out of the needs of disciplinary institutions, such as prisons and asylums, which continue to be both objects of social science inquiry and consumers of the knowledge that is produced" (Shumway and Messer-Davidow 1991, 212). But studying the social environment and secondarily applying the knowledge to alter that terrain is tantamount to annexing the site as an auxiliary laboratory. The research on those environments is generated within the academy and primarily serves academic interests. Applied research, by contrast, is generated by problems that arise outside the academy. Yet whether the research is internally or externally generated, the question that remains is, does the research serve disabled people's interests? If neither domain is informed by disabled people's perspectives, the "problems" that research is designed to address are not likely to be those that the disabled community identifies. Without disabled people's perspectives, such matters as increased public acceptance of "physician-assisted suicide,"[1] the one-dimensional representation of disability in film and in the popular press, paternalistic practices in agencies designed to assist disabled people, or noncompliance with the ADA may never be addressed.

In the creation of new fields of study, the merging across disciplines has rarely produced merging across the divide between the liberal arts and the applied fields. Fields such as sociobiology, or courses that merge literature and history, or psychology and film, marry two courses from the liberal arts. There are a few hybrid specializations within the applied fields as well, and quite recently there have been a few new specializations that do bridge the divide. Medical anthropology and sociology of health are two that not only have drawn previously isolated curricula together and generated interdisciplinary research but have also created a professional niche for graduates in hospitals and research institutions.

The in-house liberal arts mergers do help scholars, and ultimately students, think about the meaningful connections among some phenomena. However, they do little directly to prepare people to address problems raised, for example, by social influences on the study of biology. As a future politician, government worker, medical technician, lawyer, or abortion clinic supervisor, a student may benefit from the knowledge and perspectives gained in a course in history or philosophy of science. But there is no applied field that prepares people to monitor the ways social interests are served by the distribution of money for scientific research, to investigate the connections between pharmaceutical companies' research methods and social policy, or other intersections between biology and social issues such as the current climate of genetic research and its implications for prenatal screening and selective abortion. "[T]he *making* of social change does not exist as an academic inquiry" (Messer-Davidow 1991, 293). The applied fields, such as counseling, health fields, social work, and even education, are generally designed to intervene on the individual level.

Many faculty in the applied fields do attempt to bridge the gap between the liberal arts and applied fields. By training and interest, they are impelled to look into historical precedents of current practice, to refine and test psychological theory, or to conduct basic research. The applied fields, such as teacher education, where I've happily taught for the past ten years, have many faculty members who are determined to contextualize students' knowledge in philosophical, historical, scientific, or literary theories. However, we are often stymied because students expect teacher education courses to show them how to be effective teachers and liberal arts courses to supply the knowledge base they need to be informed people. The rift between the liberal arts and the applied fields, and the labeling of the applied faculty as practitioners are endemic to the institutional culture that nurtures those expectations.

SPLITS WITHIN THE APPLIED FIELDS

Another rift occurs within the applied fields, bifurcated into specialized fields and general fields. The purpose of the former is to prepare practitioners to work exclusively with people with disabilities. For instance, rehabilitation psychology and special education are specializations of psychology and of education. Students in these specializations may share few if any courses with majors in the more generalized domains, use different textbooks, and are often housed in different departments or even in different divisions.

A few universities have attempted to merge special and general education and prepare students to work in inclusive primary and secondary education settings. Syracuse University has had such a program for a number of years and also provides field placements for its student teachers in the inclusive classrooms mandated by the local Syracuse, New York, school district.

For the most part though, the study of disability is isolated in the specialized applied fields (e.g., special education, rehabilitation psychology, physical therapy), and that information is usually available only to majors in those fields. That curriculum has been developed from the perspectives of the clinician, teacher, or practitioner and perpetually casts people with disabilities in the role of patient, student, or client (Linton, Mello, and O'Neill 1995).

In teacher education, the consequences of the bifurcated system are enormous. While federal mandates are compelling schools to increase the integration of students with disabilities in general education, most teacher education programs are retaining separate systems. Although isolated courses in either teacher education program might discuss mainstreaming and, on occasion, inclusion as approaches, without actively integrating the two sets of teacher education students, these concepts appear as abstract notions.

The only justification for keeping the two programs and their respective knowledge bases separate is the idea that children with disabilities are a separate category of learner. Because special education by structure and definition places disability as the major defining variable of learners, the field overemphasizes disability, milking it for explanatory value to justify organizing education into two separate systems. Meanwhile, general education underemphasizes and marginalizes this dimension of variation in students. Therefore, neither group of teachers is adequately prepared to work in classrooms where disabled and nondisabled children can learn together (Linton 1994, 9).

Lilly (1989) predicted that special and general teacher education would merge eventually, when teacher preparation programs reflect the need to prepare teachers to work in mainstreamed schools. He notes that barriers to merger include fixed professional identities; inertia; deeply held belief systems about fundamental differences among children housed in the two systems; and the ease of "operating in one's comfort zone" (154). However, along with those obstacles, larger forces are working against dismantling this system. One is the structure of knowledge on disability as a whole in the academic curriculum, which prevents critical examination of the ideas and historical forces that perpetuate a divided society (Linton 1994). What is needed is a broad-based epistemology of inclusion, a knowledge base grounded in the liberal arts that provides the tools that academics and civilians need to make critical social, intellectual, and professional changes.

Although I am critiquing the existing structure and the dominant paradigms employed in the applied fields, it is important to recognize that disabled people's quality of life has been improved by medical, psychological, and educational intervention. There is reason to credit many in the applied fields for interventions that enhance the well-being of disabled people. Some might even argue that the disability specializations have provided the space and focus that allowed those interventions to occur. But that argument does not account for the downside of segregated training and services, which is the further sequestering of disabled people and the overdetermination of disability in those settings. Disability becomes the ring through the nose of practitioners that leads them to particular interpretations and interventions based on the idea that disability in general and specific disabilities in particular determine a constellation of psychological responses or that disabled people have such unique needs that they can be met only by specialists. This setup restricts the ability of a psychologist or teacher to place disability in a more accurate and realistic perspective.

Further, there has been minimal critical analysis within these fields of their paternalistic impulses. Work in disability studies has critiqued the tendencies of individual practitioners and institutions to assume that they know what is best for disabled people. Practices exist that limit freedom, infantilize people with disabilities, force dependency, create and perpetuate stereotypes through the use of tools such as testing and diagnosis, constrict pleasure, and limit communication and political activism among disabled people. When interventions are based on the projections and needs of professionals or are driven by maintenance of the status quo in government, medicine, or education, then disabled people have a vested interest, for our own sanity and well-being, in questioning whose interests are being served.

The generalized and specialized applied fields should integrate their programs and educate their students to view disability as a variable that should be considered in their approach to clients and students rather than as a characteristic that sets disabled people apart. Within those merged programs, advanced training in various specializations can be accomplished. A counselor with particular expertise, for instance, in pregnancy-prevention techniques for women with mobility impairments or an education specialist fluent in American Sign Language are valuable professionals, but preparing people with this type of expertise doesn't necessitate separate training programs.

Another problem with the divisions of teacher education programs into special education and general education, and counseling programs into rehabilitation and general counseling programs, is that a barrier prevents the dissemination of realistic information about disability across that divide and prevents critical examination of the medicalization of disability. Although I argue elsewhere in the book that a curriculum based on intervention and geared toward individual change is not within the province of disability studies, it is time for courses in disability studies, from a liberal arts perspective, to be introduced into the applied fields. The sociopolitical perspectives and knowledge base would force reexamination of the conceptual foundations on which the divided practice has been based, and contextualize students' knowledge of disability in the historical, philosophical, aesthetic, literary, and other bodies of knowledge that shape how they view disability and the disabled people they are to work with.

My issue is not with the existence of the applied fields, although I obviously have concerns about some of their organizing principles, it is with the dominance of the conceptualizations emanating from those fields on the study of disability. Further, at times when I or others have argued for the inclusion of disability studies in campus-wide curriculum transformation efforts, our arguments are dismissed with the explanation that the study of disability is not slighted in the academy but is covered in depth in the applied fields. But disability studies' perspectives are not present in either the liberal arts or in the applied fields.

SPLITS WITHIN THE LIBERAL ARTS

It is not only what we teach in the liberal arts, discussed in the section on content below, but where we allocate space for discussion of disability that creates problems. Lines are drawn within disciplines, parceling off particular domains of a field for the study of disability, and lines are drawn between different disciplines, blocking the entry of theoretical formulations and methodological tools from one discipline into territory commandeered by another. These two problems—splits between liberal arts disciplines, and splits within each of the disciplines—are of concern here.

An example of the latter type of split can be seen in sociology. One day I asked a faculty member in sociology whether material from lesbian and gay studies and from disability studies was represented in the department's curriculum. He said that it was; the material was covered extensively in a course required of all majors. Which course? The sociology of deviance was the not-unexpected reply. He assured me that sociologists' ideas about deviance were quite different from commonly held definitions, but I was not assured that students could avoid making that association, nor, do I suspect, can faculty. Furthermore, even if the course content is focused on deviance-making, a useful investigation for understanding the social construction of disability, the course title depicts deviance as an absolute state. In discussing such courses in "The Poverty of the Sociology of Deviance: Nuts, Sluts and Preverts," Liazos (1972) notes that their "emphasis is still on the 'deviant' and the 'problems' *he* presents to himself and others, not on the society within which he emerges and operates." Liazos then adds that textbook authors' "main concern is to *humanize* and *normalize* the 'deviant,' to show that he is essentially no different from us. But by the very emphasis on the 'deviant' . . . the opposite effect may have been achieved" (104).

Similarly, psychology reserves abnormal psychology for the major coverage of behavior and characteristics of a particular category of disabled people, those with mental illness. Other general courses, such as child development, according to the textbooks I've reviewed carefully for the past ten years, miss multiple opportunities to discuss the full range of children and their motor, sensory, social, emotional, and cognitive development. Courses in development and in each of those specific domains of development, if they discuss disability at all, describe children and adults with a range of disabilities almost exclusively in terms of pathology, deficits and abnormalities. Such textbooks could, for example, describe the similarities and differences in language development for deaf and hearing children, or discuss the ways that children with visual or mobility impairments develop their understanding of spatial relations. These and other examples could focus on which skills or abilities children rely on to accomplish these tasks, and which accommodations facilitate optimal development.

Educational psychology textbooks generally discuss children with disabilities exclusively in chapters titled "Categories of Exceptional Children," "Educating Students with Special Needs," or "Exceptional Students." The chapters often include sections on specific disabilities, with headings designating particular types of "disorders" or "impairments." The thrust of the chapters and the language used is dense with a deficit model of disability: what the child is incapable of or what the child has difficulty with, all due to disability. The remainder of the textbook is devoted to the learning abilities of the rest of the student body. It would be more fruitful to acquaint students with the skills and abilities disabled and non-disabled children use to negotiate their worlds, the similarities and differences in those capacities, and how to enhance them.

Courses in human sexuality, whether taught in psychology departments or in health education, rarely integrate information on the social, psychological, and physical components of disabled people's sexuality. If information is included on disability, it is likely to appear in separate sections or separate chapters of the textbooks, where it is primarily stated in terms of deficits or pathology. It is rare for disabled women and men to be integrated into the spectrum of human sexual behavior, interests, needs, and problems. Further, although disabled people so often report that social factors influence their sexual experience more profoundly than physiological factors, these are even less frequently discussed (Linton and Rousso 1988; Linton 1990; Waxman and Gill 1996).

Particular social science courses, such as the sociology of health, medical anthropology, and health psychology, acknowledge the presence of disability as an important variable in human communities. That focus provides an antidote to the invisibility of disability in general. Although these courses avoid some of the pathologizing stigma of abnormal psychology or the sociology of deviance, they still tend to reduce disability to a health or medical issue. That view needs to be contextualized in the scholarship that presents disability or disabled people in terms of human variation, as political category, as oppressed minority, as cultural group, or in any way that shows disability's significance as an organizing principle in human communities and in the construction of ideas about human communities. But for those courses to provide that context, the knowledge needs to be developed across the spectrum of liberal arts disciplines.

The study of science is, for the most part, kept separate from all other academic areas, a division that has been problematic for the study of disability and of women. "[F]eminists are attempting to erode the boundary between science and nonscience by claiming that the sciences are social. . . . If science is social practice, as feminists contend, then they can study it in the same ways they study other kinds of social practice" (Shumway and Messer-Davidow 1991, 210–11). Disability studies has its own bone to pick with this intractable boundary. Keeping the science and non-science domains separate and privileging medical and scientific views of disability over social and political perspectives reinforces the idea that disabled people's best hope is in the treatments and cures offered by the sciences. Further, the separation prevents interference in science's bailiwick by the meddlesome gaze of sociologists, political scientists, and historians. From a disability perspective, such endeavors as genetic testing, prenatal screening and selective abortion, determination of quality of life, and even the most basic building blocks of medicine and biology, such as the identification and labeling of symptoms and syndromes, are rife with social meaning and consequences.

Courses in the history or philosophy of science or medicine would be useful places to debunk the inviolate authority of the "empirical" fields on the study of disability and expose their investment in social agendas. If those courses were to analyze the consequences of particular philosophies, methodologies, and practices on the people labeled "patients" in their constellation, they, along with a revised sociology of health and/or medical anthropology, could be usefully incorporated into a disability studies' major.

Although the above examination of the social and hard sciences indicates the narrow, pathologized conceptualizations of disability available in that curriculum, I note that disability is, to some degree, discussed in these domains. What is absent from the curriculum is the voice of the disabled subject and the study of disability as idea, as abstract concept, and it is in the humanities that these gaps are most apparent. It is there that the meanings attributed to disability and the process of meaning-making could be examined.

Although the so-called reflective disciplines, such as philosophy, literature, some aspects of history, rhetoric, art, and history, evoke disability everywhere, they seem unable to reflect on it. It appears in treatises on the ravages of war, aesthetic theories that expound on perfect form, metaphors dripping with disability imagery, modernist notions of progress, and artistic representation of anomalous bodies. Yet, outside the disability studies literature, it is barely "unpacked." Disability has become, then, like a guest invited to a party but never introduced.

The solutions to the omissions and distortions might be found in the curriculum reform efforts taking place in the name of diversifying, democratizing, or balancing the curriculum. As we will see next, disability studies has rarely been included in those endeavors.

THE OMISSION OF DISABILITY STUDIES FROM THE MULTICULTURAL/DIVERSITY CURRICULUM

Often the debate over diversity and multicultural curriculum transformation is between those in favor of maintaining the traditional canon and those who challenge its intellectual authority. But there is another division, seemingly less politically charged because it is within the ranks of those already in favor of a more democratic and universal curriculum. That debate centers on the goals of these endeavors and the dimensions of diversity that should be represented. Both debates have a political component. They are determined by the power of the ideas as well as the power of the people putting forth the ideas. Both debates are worthwhile, but the debate within the diversity movement is less visible and the power relations among the participants not carefully examined.

Major curriculum transformation is a dynamic process; disagreement is inevitable and, in fact, desirable. But the productive dialogue is often muddied by the need to protect hard-won gains and to attain legitimacy. Henry Louis Gates, Jr. (1993) posits that the "extended face-off with conservatism has had a deforming effect, encouraging multiculturalism to know what it is against but not what it is for" (7).[2]

The terms *diversity* and *multicultural* describe various curriculum endeavors ranging from elementary school reading guides to teach empathy and acceptance of difference, to graduate seminars that utilize race, ethnicity, gender, and, at times, sexual orientation, class, and disability as analytic categories. It is not a simple linear progression, approaching the same basic ideas in increasingly sophisticated and abstract ways as the students get older. The ideas that drive these endeavors result in varied manifestations reflecting the different agendas that underlie them. Some are related to cultural diversity and teaching about differences among people; others have a more specific orientation toward exposing social and economic inequities that have determined the ways society and knowledge are configured. While much of the multicultural literature accepts "cultural appreciation as perhaps the central goal of both our classrooms and larger society, [it fails] to raise questions about prevailing political and economic arrangements. Teaching about diversity substitutes for teaching about equality, politics and the structures of oppression" (Watkins 1994, 110). The perspectives of disabled people and the field of disability studies are conspicuously absent across a broad range of endeavors, but most notably from those in the higher education curriculum and in those with a social-reconstructionist orientation.

Curriculum projects and research endeavors labeled "multicultural" or "diverse," though tremendously varied in purpose and scope, focus primarily on scholarship that analyzes race/ethnicity and gender. For numerous reasons, many still to be articulated, the construction of "multicultural" places those perspectives at the center of the discourse. The history and the consequences of that construction are for the most part invisible, giving the impression that "multiculturalism," as it is now rendered, should be the only focus of curriculum reform. Minnich (1990) in *Transforming Knowledge* states in a number of ways that it is best to focus on the "three fundamental variables of class, sex/gender, and race, for when other hierarchical distinctions have been most virulent, they have often partaken of the conceptual/emotional 'language' of race, class and gender, suggesting a basic level of significance for those three" (68). I agree that those categories have dominated the organization of knowledge in the area of curricular transformation, but I don't think that because other potential organizing structures have depended on the tools of the more frequently used categories, that creates their significance. The history of the decisions to situate those lenses in the center has yet to be written.

A number of objections have been raised to the inclusion of disability studies in that constellation; these relate to questions about the field's validity and the adequacy of its theoretical and empirical footings. People are also concerned that the diversity agenda is too inclusive and will lose its potency if the category is too elastic. These are legitimate questions, but I have not seen much active engagement with these issues. Specifically, people who either ignore the issue of disability altogether or overtly reject it as an analytic category have not, to my knowledge, actually engaged with the scholarship in their writing nor have disability studies scholars been invited to participate in plenary sessions at conferences where an open dialogue could take place. Occasionally the terms *ability* or *disability* are recited in a list of issues, but they are never discussed.

Women's studies is a significant potential site for inquiry into disability because of the many intersections between ideas about women and about disability, and because of the potential for knowledge by and about disabled people to inform women's studies. Although a large portion of the disability studies literature addresses women's issues, women's studies has been slow to recognize disabled women's issues and to integrate disability studies into its work. Thomson (1994) states that

> feminist discussions seldom include disability in their taxonomies of difference. Although ethnicity, race, and sexuality are frequently knitted into current feminist analysis, the logical leap toward seeing disability as a stigmatized social identity and a reading of the body remains largely untaken. (585)

Further, although there has been some progress in the past two years, organizations representing multicultural and diversity initiatives, cultural studies, feminist studies, lesbian and gay, queer, African American, Asian American, Native American, and Latino/Latina studies, have barely recognized disabled people's perspectives on panels or plenary sessions. Further, they have, at times, excluded disabled people by not providing access and accommodation. Although each of these fields may seem marginal, they have formed their own shape and texture and render their own authority. Therefore, the knowledge that they privilege and the knowledge they marginalize warrant consideration, particularly from the perspectives of the margins. It seems that scholars in these areas, given their struggles and their dedication to challenging privileged discourse, would welcome the types of inquiries that disability studies can provide.

The problems discussed above present a challenge to curriculum reform efforts geared toward diversifying the curriculum and to individual faculty members working to create a more accurate and representative knowledge base. The biases and points of view are usually not explicated in those endeavors, giving the appearance that the project circumscribes the only logical domain of curriculum transformation. Only a few people are talking about the social construction of "multicultural" and "diversity," and the problems and pitfalls of their construction.

For instance, Gates (1993) asks:

What is this crazy thing called multiculturalism? As an overview of the current debate suggests, a salient difficulty raised by the variety of uses to which the term has been put is that multiculturalism itself has certain imperial tendencies. Its boundaries have not been easy to establish. We are told that it is concerned with the representation of difference—but whose differences? Which differences? (6)

Gates's comments point out the inadequacy of the analysis undertaken by those involved in these endeavors. There are major aspects of theory that need to be articulated. Further, the mechanisms used, both political and intellectual, to marginalize or exclude disability studies are hidden and need to be addressed in an open forum, engaging disability studies scholars and those in the inner circle of curriculum reform. The analysis of the validity and utility of the constructs of multicultural and diversity, and the criteria for inclusion in such endeavors can benefit all concerned. The future of all such endeavors is uncertain. Some have been folded into cultural studies or even the more secular American studies. These incorporations have their own consequences for the scholarship, for curriculum transformation, and, significantly, for the types of social change that the scholarship can engender.

Whichever shape these new domains take, it is an affront that disability studies is dismissed out of hand. It is also illogical. If the lens created by these inquiries is applied to disabled people's experience and to ideas about disability, the similarities as well as the potential for unique contributions would be apparent. Disability studies shares with these other fields a number of conceptual frameworks, theoretical and ideological roots, and similar imperatives.

Moreover, incorporated into diversity initiatives, disability studies can contribute unique insights into a number of theoretical questions that arise from these endeavors. For instance, What functions do the creation of otherness, marginalization, and pathology serve in a society, and how are these processes related to the intellectual legacy of the society? How does cognitive, emotional, sensory, and physical variation relate to the formation of identity and, in turn, how do these facets of identity shape the formulation of scholarship? What are the particular intellectual and political formations that allow for a country's internal colonization of a group of people? How can current inquiries into the idea of the body be enhanced by an understanding of the social realities of people with anomalous bodies? How does group cohesion, culture, and identity form when there is no intergenerational transmission of culture, as with most lesbian and gay, and disabled people?

The structure of the curriculum also needs to be examined in terms of deeper divides and fault lines.

3. CONTENT OF CURRICULUM

What is it we say or don't say that contributes to the particular version of disability perpetrated in the academy? Is there an ableist discourse that permeates the curriculum, and if so what are its manifestations? What are the representations, dominant narratives, metaphors, and themes that contribute to ableist perspectives?

In the previous section I argued that the divisions among and within fields preclude adequate study of disability. Here I am concerned with the obstacles that exist because the present knowledge base is so steeped in a particular version of disability that it interferes with new learning. This section will examine the sciences, social sciences, and the humanities and discuss their content from the perspective of disability.

SCIENCE

Until relatively recently the sciences have steadfastly refused to examine the social meanings and the social consequences of their work. The history and impact of biology and genetics have particular salience for disabled people's lives. Other domains do not, at the moment, seem as relevant, but it may be that they have yet to be fully mined for implications for the study of disability.

Evelyn Fox Keller's work on feminist interpretations of the practice of science, particularly her analysis of the work of Barbara McClintock, is a useful starting point for thinking about the ableist constructions in the sciences. McClintock was a botanist and Nobel Prize winner about whom Keller has written extensively.

Keller (1985) notes that McClintock shared with other scientists the wish to develop "reliable (that is, shareable and reproducible) knowledge of natural order" (166). Yet McClintock's aim was not prediction, manipulation, and control but "an understanding of the world around us, that simultaneously reflects and affirms our connection to that world" (166). In her analysis, Keller challenges the subject/object split in science, the fracturing of matter into increasingly smaller and more abstract units of study, and the proclivity of science to study these units in isolation.

Research on and about disability has certainly followed the traditional path of prediction and control, subject/object split, and the study of disability in isolation from the environment. These goals are particularly apparent in recent genetics research, which has focused on prediction, and then on control, by means of prenatal screening and selective abortion, of genetically determined disabilities in the population. With geneticists' interest in and capability to study increasingly smaller and more abstracted elements of human existence, it is possible for them to distance themselves even further from the human consequences of their behavior. And, as Keller (1985) states, the "questions one asks and the explanations that one finds satisfying depend on one's a priori relation to the objects of study. . . . [T]he questions asked about objects with which one feels kinship are likely to differ from questions asked about objects one sees as unalterably alien" (167).

Scientists, the vast majority nondisabled, do their work sealed off from the critiques coming from the disabled community and from the types of analyses offered in disability studies. This screen keeps them at a distance from their ideas and also from the subjects of their investigation. In more general ways, as Keller (1985) reminds us, the objectifying lens of science is kept at a distance from the object of study by the idea that the natural world is " 'blind, simple and dumb', ontologically inferior" (167). In Keller's analysis of the relationship between ideas about science and gender, she recognizes that science has constructed the "object (nature) as female and the parallel naming of subject (mind) as male," in that "nature [is] cast in the image of woman as passive, inert, and blind" (174–75). In this picture, a number of named but unexplained terms have meanings in the science's ecology. The naming of women and the naming of nature share a history of elements that are simple and knowable, and therefore controllable. The mind (male), separate from these objects, is opaque and unknowable, and impervious to control. Keller's explanation of that fantasy provides an excellent and useful gendered reading of science. What is missing from her analysis is the meaning of the invoked terms *simple, blind,* and *dumb.* In their use in this description they appoint disability to women, but the analysis stops short of noting the gendering of disability, and the disability reading of these associations. Although I would not use *simple, blind,* or *dumb,* as intoned here, to describe anyone I know, the terms have often been used to ascribe to different groups of disabled people characteristics beyond those offered by their impairments. Keller's use of "blind, simple and dumb" is yet another incidence of the use of disability imagery as a signal to think about insentient, nonpurposeful, and ignorant behavior. In fact, the thesaurus on my computer lists *ignorant, oblivious, obtuse, unaware, irrational,* and *violent* as alternatives under *blind.*

Disabled people, like women and the natural world in general, are often rendered as passive. This idea is sustained by other ideas available both within and outside science. Consider, for instance, how terminology used for some groups of disabled people erase complexity, intentionality, and competence. *Invalid, deaf and dumb, moron, idiot,* and *wheelchair-bound* are among descriptors that inactivate the subject, making it easier to objectify and study people described in this way as specimens. Also consider how the psychoanalytic theories discussed earlier and other psychology research describe disabled people as preoccupied with their bodily states. As figures living in the body, not in the mind, disabled people are configured as childlike, even infantlike, acting on primary drives rather than engaging in purposeful behavior.

What are the consequences of thinking about disability in these ways? Consider how the scientific community, the media, and society in general have embraced technological breakthroughs in prenatal screening and the "solutions" found in selective abortion. Attempting to eradicate disability or foolishly believing that it is possible to do so are an action and intention with consequences for the lived experience of disabled people. These impulses may be driven by modernist goals of progress and perfection. The remaining disabled people, those who slip in unchecked, repudiate the scientific wizardry and run the risk, as we always have, of receiving the displaced anger of the frustrated doctors and their devoted followers.

The pointed and provocative questions that some disability studies scholars are asking genetic researchers is, Are you saying my life is not worth living, that I should not have been born, that I don't have a place in your version of the world? The enormous amount of money the government is giving to the Human Genome Project to identify genetic markers for disability stands in contrast to the money provided to existing disabled people.

Scientists and society at large are unused to disabled people as assertive, active, and, at times, aggressive. They are not used to disabled people who have little interest in being cured or in eliminating disability. If scientists reckon with that active voice, they may begin to see the disabled subject as less passive and controllable. The active voice of disabled people and the activated subject have a place in a comprehensive and representative science curriculum.

A revisioned science curriculum should direct attention to the place of disability in the environment, its meaning and function. Barbara McClintock's research, also discussed in chapter 5, on the relation of anomalous characteristics or members of the species to the whole, points the way toward conceptualizing disability as a piece of the puzzle, a part of the fiber of life. Science and medicine might turn their attention to the useful, necessary, or adaptive aspects of disability or maybe even the irrelevant or neutral aspects. Another McClintock, Martha, a professor of biopsychology at the University of Chicago, may also have something to offer. She is overseeing the construction of an institute and laboratory to study the link between environment and biology, where the "focus will be on a top-down approach to understanding biology—going from the whole organism toward the innermost layer of the gene—rather than the standard bottom-up, beginning with the gene and looking outward" (Angier 1995, C5). These ideas will service disabled people only if scientists invite a disability reading of their work. That reading will service science only if theory begins to knit disability into the fabric of life, thread by thread, idea by idea.

SOCIAL SCIENCES

Psychology, anthropology, economics, political science, sociology and history are useful disciplines from which to examine disability. Each of these fields provides the research tools and theoretical material needed to shed light on disability as a social construct and on the manifestations and consequences of particular constructions. The behaviors, social practices, economic implications, political mechanisms, and cultural functions related to disability are potentially part of a representative curriculum. Yet within each field, in practice, the potential is unrealized because existing ideas about disability and discipline-specific conventions preclude adequate study.

In a number of respects, disability is studied more consciously and deliberately as effect rather than cause. Disability is understood best as a tragic consequence of war, fate, modern technology, God's will, poverty, or the failure of medicine's omnipotence. Rendered as effect rather than cause, disability is inactivated and muted. It is assumed to be something to be avoided or eliminated and, when it exists, to be cured or ameliorated—something to be acted on or reacted to. When depicted as causal agents, disability or disabled people are most often studied in a deterministic manner, as the predictor variable; this holds for studies of individuals' response to their own disability, studies of nondisabled people's response to disabled people, and the broader evaluation of various societies' responses to disability. It is rare for human variation, and the particular configurations called disabilities, to be studied as variables situated in a web of other variables.

Consider, for instance, the prevailing ideas about the relationships that disabled people have to their disabilities. In psychology, many of these ideas are filed in the category loosely called "adjustment literature," whose focus on individual adjustment reinforces the idea that disability is an individual problem requiring individual interventions. In the case of acquired disabilities, those that occur after birth, the relationship is described in terms of people's adjustment *to* their disabilities. What is missing in this picture are the myriad adjustments *following* disability. Although the idea of adjustment is inadequate to describe the shifts in identity, community, culture, role, and experience that often take place following the onset of significant disability, the latter phrase at least provides space for the investigation of some of the social transformations and adaptations that occur. The onset of disability initiates intrapsychic adjustments not only to changes in bodily configuration and functioning, to sensory loss, or to shifts in emotional or cognitive makeup but to concomitant changes in others' perceptions of the disabled person, in role expectations, in social positioning, in her or his place in the family constellation, and in access to educational, economic, and social opportunities. The dynamic relationship among all these variables is the climate *following* the onset of disability. Attempting to isolate and study the individual's intrapsychic adjustment *to* disability from that mix is extremely difficult.

Studies that attempt to do so overdetermine disability itself, assigning far too much weight to it. Instead, if the contextual contingencies were evaluated to determine their contribution in shaping response to disability, we might learn more about the ways that the availability of accessible transportation, social opportunities, employment options, and other factors relate to the experience of disability. It would be more useful to study the degree of fit of the individual in the environment as a predictor of adaptation rather than adjustment.

The psychoanalytic literature also has a deterministic bent with respect to the study of people's response to disability. Harris and Wideman (1988) write that "classical psychoanalytic thought treats disability as a precursor to narcissistic disorders, and a compromise to very early primary narcissism. . . . [T]he individual's experience of disability is viewed only as a negative aspect of self-image, as a defense against genetic weakness, almost inherently and inevitably a feature of the individual's psychic life" (117). In several places over the years the psychoanalytic literature has posited that disabled people's need to attend to bodily functions drains psychic energy, causing narcissistic preoccupation with the self and resulting in immaturity and difficulty forming adequate object relations.

Alfred Adler put forth a deterministic argument in his ideas about compensation for feelings of inferiority. Although he came to see all humans as struggling with feelings of inferiority, he developed the idea based on interest in those with "organ inferiority." Coleman and Croake (1987) accept Adler's idea uncritically. They conducted research on "twenty-six children . . . randomly selected from the Bureau of Crippled Children rolls" (367) to determine their tendency toward "overcompensation." To set the stage for reporting their findings, they provide examples of people whom they describe as "overcompensating" for "their defective organs": "Demosthenes, who had a speech impediment and became known for his great oration, and Franklin Roosevelt, who was crippled by polio-myelitis, and became president of the U.S." (364). The authors see the accomplishments of these famous men and of the children in their study solely as a function of "compensation" for their disabilities.

Although psychoanalytic theorists have speculated about the psychopathology and ego deficits in people with disabilities, particularly those with congenital or early-onset disabilities, they haven't been so ready to propose a means to apply their theories toward addressing these problems. "Much psychoanalytic literature on disability supports the contention that the disabled are inherently unanalyzable" (Asch and Rousso 1985, 4). This stance has presented particular obstacles to disabled women and men seeking psychoanalytic training because psychoanalysis is a prerequisite or corequisite for such professional training.

Feminist critiques of the psychoanalytic literature have exposed interpretations that render the female as weak, envious, immature, and driven by emotions. Antidisability messages similarly run rampant in the literature; passivity, immaturity, narcissistic preoccupation of disabled people, and the overpowering influence of disability as psychic determinant are entrenched ideas. Further, reading the psychoanalytic literature with a combined feminist and disability lens reveals likenesses in the attributions of symptoms and characteristics. This combined reading yields information on the feminization of disability and the construction of the female as disabled in this literature.

Disabled people's views on disability often challenge fundamental psychoanalytic precepts. Explicating the neutral, ordinary, and even the positive aspects of the disability experience that many disabled people have expressed is akin to debunking the myth of penis envy. It is often startling to nondisabled people that many disabled people do not pine for the nondisabled experience, nor do they conceptualize disability as a potent determinant of their experience. Although women often report envying the status and privilege of men, and disabled people would celebrate the day of attaining equal social status, these are social and political determinants, not intrapsychic ones.

In the social psychology literature, there appears to be a similarly narrow range of explanations of the disability experience. A large body of research, often called attitude research, has looked mostly at nondisabled people's attitudes toward disabled people. In this picture, disability is the causal agent, bringing about a response that is mediated by the personal and demographic characteristics of nondisabled people, which are said to relate to the quality and intensity of the response. It is as if disability and disabled people have been assigned a particular weight and valence that everyone agrees upon, and then what gets measured is the variation in nondisabled people that results in different responses. Hirsch (1995) critiques Goffman's position in *Stigma,* one of the most widely used theoretical approaches, because it "assumes that in Western cultures a disability will always be interpreted as a stigma for the individual to cope with" (10).

Yet the weight and valence assigned to disability are not fixed; they are the products of the prevailing belief systems, social positioning of disabled people, the rights and freedoms accorded to disabled people at the time and place of the study, the degree of integration of disabled people in the community, and a host of other tangible and intangible factors. Those contingencies are rarely studied. Further, the preponderance of attitude research on nondisabled people's response to disability as a function of their anxiety, racism, socioeconomic status, and so on yields data of limited utility. Without information on the contextual variables in order to use these results to better the situation of disabled people, one would have to design individual interventions to alter the personal characteristics of those with negative attitudes. The glut of this one-way attitude research prompted one of my friends (a disabled woman), while we were sitting in the audience at a conference presentation, to whisper to me, "I'm tired of hearing how they feel about us. Why doesn't anybody ask how we feel about them!"

Moreover, these studies primarily measure the source and quality of negative attitudes. In psychology, personal attitudes are studied; in sociology and anthropology, studies of deviance or the deviant are in order. Bogdan and Taylor (1987) have formulated a *sociology of acceptance* in response to the focus in sociology over the past twenty-five years "on stigma and the labeling and rejection of people with negatively valued physical, mental, and behavioral differences (deviant, different, or atypical) . . . resulting in a sociology of exclusion" (34). Their approach enables sociologists to study integration, acceptance, and nonstigmatized relationships also.

Anthropology and history are two areas of scholarship that could paint a broader picture of disability. Scheer and Luborsky (1991) define anthropology as the "cross-cultural and holistic social science, [which] analyzes how the interaction between cultural values and beliefs, social relations, and historical changes affect patterns of daily life and personal experience" (1173). The dynamic interaction proposed in anthropology's mission could yield important data for the study of disability. Disability culture is a critical conceptual framework in disability studies scholarship for discussing the shared aspects of our experience, and the language, customs, and artistic products that emerge from that experience. To the degree that disabled people's culture moderates or overrides the cultural expectations and norms of the dominant group, anthropologists need to be alert to it. John Hockenberry (1995), a reporter who spent a considerable amount of time in the Middle East, talks about the ways that his experiences as a disabled person differ from the dominant American culture he was raised in:

> Americans expect things to work. It is one of the consequences of being a superpower. Disabled people expect things not to work whether they are American or not. In Israel and the occu-

pied territories I shared no language or religion with the people I met. To my surprise, I discovered that we shared a world view that had always isolated me in the United States. (263)

For anthropology to address disability adequately, the field would have to attend to the "daily life and personal experience" of disabled people more systematically and deliberately than it has in the past, and would have to do so in the context of the "cultural values" and other factors that shape experience. Few anthropologists have systematically studied disabled peoples' experience, habits, customs, in-group and out-group behavior, stories, and imagery, and fewer still have done so from the perspective of disabled people themselves. Groce and Scheer (1990) blame the lack on the commonly held assumption that "in pre-industrial and traditional societies, disabled individuals are not able to, or are not allowed to live past early childhood" (v). They refute this assumption and note that existing data do not support those contentions.

The pervasiveness of the assumption helps explain the minimal attention anthropologists have given to the study of disability in traditional societies, but a more entrenched problem may be the adherence in the field to traditional definitions of culture that are dependent on intergenerational transmission of values, beliefs, customs, and other aspects of a culture. That tenet structures most anthropological research and interferes with adequate study of lesbian and gay, and disability cultures. In these groups, identification often does not start until adolescence or adulthood, so the culture is transmitted largely by adults to other adults. Even at that time, many disabled people are discouraged by their families from socializing with or allying with other disabled people; more troubling, disabled people may internalize the norms and values of the society and shun other disabled people for fear that they will be identified with the socially marginal group. Nevertheless, despite these tensions and despite some intragroup conflicts, the disability community has become, particularly over the past twenty-five years, strong and cohesive.

Another major limitation of anthropology is the absence of the active voice of disabled people as researchers and as subjects. For the most part, even studies such as the Hankses' research discussed in chapter 3, which have examined various societies to ascertain how disabled people are treated or what the prevailing beliefs are about disability, evaluate the dominant, nondisabled majority's perspectives and behavior. One interpretation of the absence of disabled people's perspectives is that disabled people are marginalized in most societies; most important, the society from which the researcher herself or himself comes from. Hence, the researcher enters the environment unprepared to find disabled people's perspectives a valuable indicator of "cultural values and beliefs." Further, ethnocentric bias, meaning in this case the researcher's likely nondisabled status, influences how particular practices related to disability are interpreted.

There is a tendency in anthropology and in other fields to view response to disability and accommodation of disabled people as a function of the scientific expertise and perceived social advancement of a culture rather than as a product of the cultural norms and expectations, and the disability politics. In doing so, there is a valorization of Western practices and of the perspectives of the late twentieth century. Anthropology can look to its own history of internal self-study for the tools to correct this bias. In the nineteenth century and early twentieth, anthropology played an active role in colonialism. "Anthropology, and its modes of inquiry, became particularly useful during the period of colonial exploration and conquest. Colonizers could come to know the alien behavior of those they were to exploit and subjugate" (Watkins 1994, 106). Anthropologists participated by providing knowledge about the people to be subjugated and by presenting the colonialists' ventures in the best possible light. By masking the controlling and violent nature of the colonial process, anthropology contributed to the idealization of colonialism's mission.

The heightened self-consciousness of the postcolonial moment makes anthropology an excellent location to examine how its formulations and practices interfere with accurate representation of disability in the curriculum and influence disability policy and practice. Anthropology has done one of the most rigorous self-studies of any field, critiquing its role in the process of colonization of non-Western countries. Reflecting further on its own history, the field should examine how scholarship valorizes practices that include containment and control of disabled people—in other words, the colonization of disabled people—within our own shores. Disabled people have voiced objection to institutionalization, to the medical control over activities and services that could be transferred to community leadership, and to the eclipse of disability perspectives by professionals. Institutions and asylums—several of which were called "The Colony" earlier in this century—replicate some of the patterns of control and containment that have earned colonization on foreign shores its bad name.

Postcolonial perspectives offer anthropologists insights into "the demand to speak rather than being spoken for and to represent oneself rather than being represented or, in the worst cases, rather than being effaced entirely" (Frank 1995, 13). As one example of the potential of such an analysis, Frank, in *The Wounded Storyteller*, contrasts those "willing to continue to play the medical 'patient' game by modernist rules without question," with "post-colonial members of the remission society . . . refusing to be reduced to 'clinical material' in the construction of the medical text, they are claiming voices" (12).

I suggest that anthropology examine the consequences of studying disability almost exclusively through the lens of the dominant, nondisabled majority. The majority position is likely to emphasize the benevolent and enlightened impulses that guide prevailing practices. Cross-cultural data could yield significant information on commonalities, patterns, and historical trends in response to disability in the same way that cross-cultural information on women has yielded rich data that support understanding of patterns of male dominance. Medical anthropology's role in this examination is extremely important, but it is the broader field of anthropology that must locate disability's place in the cultures studied. Last, anthropology needs to analyze how marginalizing the study of disability in any environment observed contributes to the marginalization of disabled people in those cultures, as well as in the culture where the research is disseminated.

History is another domain where the lack of recognition of disability as a structuring element of a society and where the elevation of contemporary Western ideals compromise the knowledge base. As those who are engaged in formulating social history have reminded us, the removal or marginalization of the lives and contributions of vast number of people from the annals of history has created a lopsided view of the past. Hirsch (1995) explains the absence of the perspectives and contributions of disabled people as a function of fear, "individual fear of losing bodily worth and function, and societal fear that a large number of disabled individuals might somehow endanger the future of the human species" (6).

In addition, other forces act against noting disability as an issue and disabled people as a constituency. One is that most cultures construct disability as an "individual problem," which works against viewing disability through the lens of history. Whether the culture's tendency to individualize disability is a result of privileging religious explanations or medical explanations of disability, both result in reduced attention to a society's practices with respect to disability. Another problem is that any country whose history is being chronicled may mask disability in its populace in order to present an image of a "healthy" state. For instance, in late-eighteenth-century France, "both the popular press and political elite

DIVIDED CURRICULUM

ushered in by the Revolution saw a direct parallel between the reform of the body politic and the health of the physical body of the French citizen" (Mirzoeff 1995, 49).

Paul Longmore (1985b) makes a convincing argument that "the history of disabled people as a distinct minority remains largely unwritten and unknown" and demonstrates how that obscurity has compromised understanding of figures such as Randolph Bourne and their contributions to history (586). He urges "historians . . . [to] apply a minority group analysis to the historical experience of disabled people" because "when devaluation and discrimination happen to one person, it is biography, but when, in all probability, similar experiences happened to millions, it is social history" (586).

Hirsch (1995) recommends collecting oral histories of disabled people as a means to trace commonalities in experience. She cautions, however, that these oral histories will not serve the purpose if they do not relate people's stories to historical events or time periods. Past interviews have served only to "reinforce a notion of individual coping and personal adjustments. . . . This kind of disaggregation of the group into isolated individuals does not seem to happen to other groups whose cultural connections and historical significance are being portrayed through oral history collections" (9).

Further, all research that is conducted after the fact on scientific, historical, or cultural materials tends to impose contemporary ideas about disability on interpretations of past practices. These studies are designed to make sense of, to interpret, evidence in a new way. For instance, the theoretical tools of psychoanalysis have been applied to literary works and historical documents to produce psychoanalytic studies of the novel, the novelist, and of historical figures. Another example might be the analysis of archaeological findings from various disciplinary perspectives used to construct a picture of ancient societies.

When these interpretive lenses have been focused on disability, the studies rarely contribute to a social or political analysis of disability. There is variation, however. For example, different researchers have arrived at different interpretations of paleontological evidence. Trinkhaus and Shipman (1993) describe the fossil remains of a Neanderthal male who is believed to have sustained serious injuries that resulted in impaired mobility, partial blindness, and the use of only one arm. He lived for thirty to forty-five years, a long life span. The authors comment that his survival was due to the "compassion" and "humanity" of the Neanderthals. Stephen Jay Gould (1988) describes an individual from the Upper Paleolithic period whose remains indicate physical disabilities (a form of dwarfism resulting in limited mobility) that would have restricted his participation in the hunting and gathering activities, and the nomadic life of his group. The man was buried in a cave that appeared to be a burial site for people of high status. Gould speculates that his social standing may have afforded him this honor, or that his differences were valued, or that "his deeds or intelligence won respect despite his physical handicaps" (18).

Scheer and Groce (1988) have also reviewed information on prehistoric life and critique the narrow and stereotypical interpretations of the evidence generally found in contemporary scholarship. They note that in prehistoric societies, people with disabilities existed in greater numbers than current evidence suggests. They compare interpretations of those data with interpretations of the situation of people with disabilities in contemporary nonindustrialized societies and refute some commonly held assumptions that "disabled individuals born outside the industrialized world were either killed at birth or died when young" (24). Although these practices did and continue to occur, there is tremendous variation among them and in the value systems that determine them. Scheer and Groce note how scholars in the United States tend to glorify the modern industrialized nations' treatment of people with disabilities, and that tendency shapes interpretations of data. For instance, they quote *Human Evolution,* a standard textbook on biological anthropology (Birdsell 1972): "Biologically handicapped children are a humanistic concern in our society whereas in simple human populations they died early and were not missed" (384). Scheer and Groce argue for analysis of the social construction of disability within a given society, as well as analysis of the reconstruction that takes place in scholarship as meaning is accorded to data collected about that society.

Nichols (1993), looking not at paleontological evidence but at data from ethnographic studies, also comments on the varied interpretations of traditional societies that exist in contemporary scholarship. He attempts in writing about traditional African attitudes toward disability to counteract the "observable tendency to reduce African ideas about disability to a few hackneyed scenarios whereby disability is seen either as a result of witchcraft . . . or as a form of divine retribution" (26). He notes that modern industrialized societies tend to dismiss African ideas as "barbaric" or "primitive." Instead, he differentiates between African belief systems based on "*pragmatic spirituality* that reflect[s] knowledge and utility, and *blind superstition* which is in bondage to ignorance" (Nichols's italics), in order to demonstrate the human and humane ideas that inform many African approaches to disability (29).[3] In focusing solely on mystical interpretations, the researcher may not only bypass the practical explanations of disability inherent in the culture's philosophy but also ignore the society's practical responses. Studying traditional societies' mechanisms for accommodating disabled people may yield insights into the positive aspects of local solutions, some of which may afford greater freedom and rights to disabled people than those available in societies with a strong institutional culture.

Women's studies, lesbian and gay studies, disability studies and a range of other new scholarship have challenged all the disciplines to evaluate the adequacy of their explanatory power in the face of the glaring omissions that have recently been exposed. Each social science discipline needs to evaluate the validity and utility of its field and consider the configuration of the social sciences in general for responding to the questions raised by a disability inquiry. One way of conceptualizing past social science research on disability is as a kind of damage control. Particularly, research in the prediction and control mode of social science has been aimed at reducing the incidence of disability, reducing the impact of disability on the individual, or reducing the negative impact of disability on society. It may seem foolish to take issue with such an agenda. After all, isn't reduction of disability everyone's aim? Maybe not. What I find most troubling about the impulse to eliminate, cure, or contain disability is the ascendancy of that idea over accommodation and integration. The impulse to control disability rather than to stop oppression is the theme throughout the social science literature that is most problematic and most in need of problematizing.

HUMANITIES AND THE ARTS

The study of literature, linguistics, philosophy, art, aesthetics and literary criticism, and all areas of the arts dances around disability but rarely lights on it. Disability imagery abounds in the materials considered and produced in these fields, and yet because it is not analyzed, it remains as background, seemingly of little consequence. Disability, as perspective, has rarely been employed to flush out the hidden themes, images, metaphors, and problematic elements of the fields' guiding philosophies.

As I look broadly across the humanities and the arts, I see an array of problems that affect not only what we as a society know about disability but how we act with respect to disability. I have chosen two broad, conceptual errors that I see as particularly potent, in part because they are largely invisible. This is a starting point, not an exhaustive analysis.

The first error is the idea that disabled and nondisabled people have differing capacities and entitlements when it comes to pleasure. This idea functions in different ways. Disabled people, across all disability groups, are thought to have compromised "pleasure systems." The capacity to engage in pleasurable activity—experiences sought for their own sake, for the stimulation and enjoyment they provide—is assumed to be out of reach of the disabled. Although it may be recognized that disabled people seek such activity, their doing so is conceptualized as mere compensation for the void created by disability. This notion is fed by deterministic arguments that accord tremendous weight to disability, in effect saying that it eclipses pleasure, joy, and, to an extent, creativity. As a result, disabled people seeking pleasurable experiences are thought to be searching for something to soothe, to comfort, or to take their mind off their troubles rather than something to activate the imagination, heighten awareness, or to spur themselves on to social change.

Society's choice, and I see it as a choice, to exclude disabled people from social and cultural events that afford pleasure, to deny them sex education, sexual health care, and, at times, marriage, privacy, and friendship are indications of the belief that pleasure is less consequential to disabled people than to nondisabled people. Yet that belief is likely a rationalization for more virulent impulses. Are disabled people denied access to pleasure by the unspoken notion that they are not entitled to it because they cause displeasure to others? The body of the cripple, the sensory impairment of the deaf and blind, the idiosyncratic functioning of people with mental illness cause displeasure to those accustomed to disdain and disparage these characteristics. How dare we crippled, blind, and crazy folks ask for parity? Shouldn't we be satisfied with the provision of medical care and sustenance, and leave the luxuries for those who are thought to drain fewer resources from society?

Although there have been class, gender, race, and age analyses of the way society structures access to pleasure, there have not been similar disability analyses. As a result inadequate attention has been given to the ways disabled people are denied pleasure, not by the vagaries of their conditions but by the notion that they would muddy up frivolity, joy, and delight, take away from the purity of precious moments.

The humanities and the arts can benefit from an analysis of who in society is believed to be entitled to pleasure and who is thought to have the capacity to provide pleasure. These themes and issues can be employed in analysis of how characters in fiction, film, and theater are depicted as draining pleasure from others or are themselves compromised in their ability to experience pleasure. These ideas can be used to evaluate the philosophical underpinnings of architectural design or urban planning, exploring how utilitarian versus aesthetic considerations dominate in approaches to accessible environments. Philosophy can consider how the idea that pleasure is related to ideals of beauty, and physical and psychological perfection seeps unchecked into commonly held belief systems. The potential exists throughout the humanities and the arts for curriculum to humanize disability, to neutralize it and make it less opaque, terrifying, and alienating. I have chosen pleasure not so much as a location for work that needs to be done but as a route or point of departure for work that could be done.

Another theme or issue that the humanities and arts can investigate is the many ways that curricula and artistic products render disability as powerful and disabled people as powerless. The imbalance is fed by deterministic arguments that place disability as the overwhelming force in people's existence. There are a number of ways that our culture portrays disabled people as victims of disability, most notably in using *victim* to describe people who have particular conditions, such as "The woman is a victim of cerebral palsy." The disability in this depiction wipes out the person, the person's intentionality and potential control of her life. Even a semifictional character whose behavior is shown as purposeful, such as Shakespeare's Richard III, is characterized as acting on his un-controllable aggressive urges because, as he tells us in the opening monologue, that because he cannot

> prove a lover,
> To entertain these fair well-spoken days,
> I am determined to prove a villain
> And hate the idle pleasures of these days.

His disability, he asserts, has rendered him incapable of sexual and pleasurable pursuits. He, his nephews, and other "victims" suffer at the hands of his ferocious disability.

In some ways the theme of disability as powerful agent and the disabled individual as hapless or helpless victim can be seen in the assignment of the study of disability to the applied fields, with minor incursions in the social science curriculum and insignificant representation in the humanities. Disability is, in this configura-tion, something to do something about, to control and make less potent, not something to understand and interpret. Disabled peo-ple are those to be provided for, given to, and helped. Reading the narrative of the curriculum as a whole, disability is something to take action on, not something to reflect on. Yet, although disabled people are victims, not actors in the story, disability itself has agency, intention, and power.

In considering how we can redress these conceptual errors and the many others still to be articulated, a critical element is attending to the active voice of the artist, writer, and theorist with a personal disability perspective. Particularly noteworthy for its absence is the voice that speaks not of shame, pain, and loss but of life, delight, struggle, and purposeful action. Writers are needed who can dem-onstrate that success in terms of disability is more than a personal triumph over physical adversity; it is a life that consciously reckons with the social forces that oppress and control. The writer who demonstrates that for many disabled people, oppression is not experienced as a bodily force but a political force.

Literary criticism has not done a very good job of challenging the dominant disability narratives. Analyses are needed, similar to those that have been done on the self-loathing homosexual figures in the *Boys in the Band,* or of passive, meek women in stereotypical roles. Where is the critique of the aching narrative of the blind man or of the crippled man, trapped in a pitiable body, the body he says has betrayed him? Not only have these characters been written of predominantly by nondisabled women and men, those same authors don't also write the stories of disabled people comfortable in their skins, those for whom disability is an integral but not despised element of life.

Nancy Mairs (1996) talks of the need for voices in her review of Michael Bérubé's (1996) *Life as We Know It: A Father, a Family, and an Exceptional Child* and identifies Bérubé as one of those voices:

> The mediated picture of disabled life is so untrue to that life's realities as to encourage the view that people with disabilities constitute sores on the social body to be eradicated rather than the ordinary wens and freckles to which any flesh is heir. To counteract such a view requires voices—linguistically sophisticated, intellectually nuanced and politically astute—capable of articulating the issues raised by the full inclusion of people with disabilities in society. (30)

I have also seen in the past few years, a number of actors, performance artists, poets, and dancers with a range of disabilities who take on these issues. They often use their bodies or life experiences to confront stereotypes and to depict the peculiar ways that outsiders' respond to disabled people. They also represent experience from the insider's viewpoint in candid, often hilarious, charged, and confrontational ways.[4] So often thought by our very existence to transgress moral or aesthetic standards, disabled people in these events purposefully transgress social standards. For any significant curricular or social change to take place, radicalizing voices such as these will need to be admitted into the canon.

In this chapter I have examined the limitations of the dominant curriculum with respect to the accurate representation of disability: the structure and content of the curriculum, and the methods of inquiry employed each contribute to misinformation, and gaps and weaknesses in the knowledge base. In its placement of disability inquiries in the specialized applied fields, the curriculum medicalizes and individualizes disability. In restricting representation of disability issues to pathologized quadrants of the curriculum, it reinforces the idea that disability is deviant and undesirable, for an individual or a society. Disability is a thing to be avoided and contained rather than an inevitable part of life that can be responded to more effectively and positively. The absence of meaningful inquiry in the humanities compounds this problem. The curriculum is devoid of the types of interpretative research and analyses that could shed light on the preponderance of malignant and unsavory imagery in the curriculum and in cultural products. Disability studies, which is examined in the next chapter, provides the means to redress these faults.

NOTES

1. I prefer to use the term *euthanasia*. The currently popular term *physician-assisted suicide* is not accurate to describe the deaths of people who are vulnerable to coercion because of economic necessity, family or social pressure, or disability. In those situations, vulnerable people may be agreeing to death to satisfy others' needs, not their own.

2. Gates' use of *deforming* in this context appears to me to have more to do with a disassembling process than a disabling one, and yet

images of disabled people as incomplete, not fully formed, or "disassembled" are important ideas to analyze as well.

3. It is unfortunate that Nichols used *blind* to modify superstition and to contrast it to *pragmatic*. This construction reinforces the idea that blindness indicates lack of knowledge, randomness, and primitive reasoning.

4. An excellent source for this material is the video "Vital Signs: Crip Culture Talks Back" (1996) created by Sharon Snyder and David Mitchell. It is available from Brace Yourselves Productions, Northern Michigan University, Marquette, Michigan 49855.

5

ENTER DISABILITY STUDIES

> [O]ne group's perspective on knowledge has set the terms of human understanding. This includes how best to achieve knowledge and how to distinguish between good and bad knowledge.
>
> Sampson 1993, 1225

> [I]f disabled people and their knowledge were fully integrated into society, everyone's relation to her/his real body would be liberated.
>
> Wendell 1989, 104

As with many of the new interdisciplinary fields, creating the category "disability studies" didn't create the scholarship. Instead, the name organizes and circumscribes a knowledge base that explains the social and political nature of the ascribed category, disability. The formal establishment of the field provided a structure for research and theory across the disciplines focused on disability as a social phenomenon, a perspective largely ignored or misrepresented in the curriculum.

The social, political, and cultural analyses undertaken by disability studies form a prism through which one can gain a broader understanding of society and human experience, and the significance of human variation. As Longmore noted in a personal communication in 1992, disability studies deepens the "historical comprehension of a broad range of subjects, for instance the history of values and beliefs regarding human nature, gender and sexuality; American notions of individualism and equality, and the social and legal definition of what constitutes a minority group."

A disability studies perspective adds a critical dimension to thinking about issues such as autonomy, competence, wholeness, independence/dependence, health, physical appearance, aesthetics, community, and notions of progress and perfection—issues that pervade every aspect of the civic and pedagogic culture. They appear as themes in literature, as variables in social and biological science, as dimensions of historical analysis, and as criteria for social policy and practice. Scholarship in this field addresses such fundamental ideas as who is considered a burden and who a resource, who is expendable and who is esteemed, who should engage in the activities that might lead to reproduction and who should not, and, if reproduction is not the aim, who can engage in erotic pleasures and who should not.[1]

Reference lists, particularly in the past few years, sweep across the disciplines, capturing and organizing work from seemingly disparate areas. The body of work includes authors who identify disability studies as their area of scholarship, and also others who are peripheral to the field. For example, such well-circulated texts as Susan Sontag's (1978) *Illness as Metaphor,* Stephen Jay Gould's (1981) *Mismeasure of Man,* and Sander Gilman's (1985) *Difference and Pathology* and the works of Thomas Szasz, Michel Foucault, and Oliver Sacks have served a critical function in the formulation of theory. Yet these authors probably do not identify with disability studies, and indeed may never have heard of the field.

Another group that has contributed to disability studies scholarship includes writers in other domains who have deliberately incorporated disability in their thinking. For instance, Ruth Hubbard's

(1990) *Politics of Women's Biology* investigates disability issues in the chapter "Who Should Inhabit the World?" which looks at the way prejudice against disabled people is implemented when "scientists and physicians are making the decisions about what lives to 'target' as not worth living" (198). She believes that the public participates by accepting, even "hail[ing] as progress tests that enable us to try to avoid having children with disabilities" (179). She supports women's right to terminate a pregnancy but emphasizes that women "must also feel empowered not to terminate it, confident that the society will do what it can to enable her and her child to live fulfilling lives" (197). Iris Marion Young's (1990) *Justice and the Politics of Difference* examines how theories of social justice omit discussion of social-group differences, and group differences in power and privilege. Young incorporates ableism as one of many perspectives of the dominant group that has social and legal consequences and describes its impact on disabled people. Minow (1990) actively incorporates disability issues in her examination of the legal treatment of difference. Her work contributes to an understanding of the process of "difference-making" by shifting the focus from the "distinctions [made] between people to a focus on the relationships within which we notice and draw distinctions" (15). Christine Sleeter and Carl Grant's (1991) study of race, class, gender, and disability in textbooks specifies disability as a meaningful aspect of diversity, analyzes existing representations, and documents its underrepresentation.

But it is the authors who deliberately set out to place ideas about disability in more specifically contingent relationships to the social situation of disabled people and to the disability rights movement who form the core group of disability studies scholars. Many in this group view the establishment of disability studies as part of an overt agenda to gain power for disabled people through organizing and coalescing people, resources, and knowledge.

ENTER DISABILITY STUDIES

GOALS

A goal right now for this field is to formulate the epistemological foundation for viewing disability as a critical category of analysis, the absence of which weakens the knowledge base. To further that process, I've delineated four areas for future research. My aim here is to draw from within and outside disability studies to point the way toward a more comprehensive articulation of disability studies epistemology than has previously been undertaken. Increased attention to these four domains can assist in the formulation of the ideas that have explanatory and transformational value for the curriculum as a whole.

1. Theories are needed across the curriculum that conceptualize disabled and nondisabled people as complementary parts of a whole integrated universe. Ideas from several domains can contribute to these formulations. Evelyn Fox Keller's (1985) analysis of the work of Barbara McClintock, a geneticist born at the beginning of the twentieth century, is a good start. Although I don't believe that McClintock ever directly addressed the sciences' construction of disability, her interest in the exceptional case in genetic research and her respect for individual difference and complexity stand in contrast to the typical bifurcation of characteristics or people into normal and abnormal. McClintock believed that rather than dismiss as aberrant members of a species that stray from the norm, it is more useful to see difference as "evidence not of lawlessness or disorder but of a larger system of order, one that cannot be reduced to a single law" (164). In an interview, McClintock said, "If [something] doesn't fit, there's a reason and you find out what it is." Rather than overlook difference, for instance, by naming an anomalous kernel of corn "an exception, an aberration, a contaminant," she worked to understand its place and function. Keller adds that "difference constitutes a principle for ordering the world radically, unlike the principle of division or dichotomization. . . . [Whereas] division severs connection and imposes distance; the

recognition of difference provides a starting point for relatedness . . ." (163). Two articles have addressed applications of McClintock's ideas for thinking about disability. In a piece I wrote with colleagues (Linton, Mello, and O'Neill 1994), we point out how McClintock's ideas can inform ethical debates related to eliminating difference through the use of prenatal screening and selective abortion, forced sterilization, or euthanasia. Minow (1990) found in the work of McClintock insights for her study on conceptions of difference in the American legal system. Minow comments on McClintock's "attention to relationships between parts and wholes and between the observer and the observed" (202). These ideas are useful, not to attempt to erase difference but to look at the consequences of the way difference is understood and acted upon.

The key to the formulation of theory is to examine, as McClintock did, the complementarity and interdependence of parts to wholes. This involves recognition of disabled and nondisabled people as distinct groups, the relationship of one to the other, and of both to the social structures in which they function.

2. Disability studies needs to articulate how and in what areas of theory centering disability perspectives can be advantageous for knowledge development in all content areas. McCagg and Siegelbaum (1989) take on a piece of this project in their study of the disabled in the Soviet Union, in which they consider ways that the "fate of the disabled . . . provides clues to the inner directions of modern society" (3). They explain that the "fate of the disabled [has] this weather vane character . . . [because] societies always reveal themselves through their treatment of the helpless among their own populations." Their effort to center disability as a pivotal point of analysis is worthwhile but falls short because they believe disabled people's oppression comes from "the conditions nature has imposed on them" (6) rather than from the socioeconomic, political, and cultural oppression that other marginalized groups experience. If they were to step further back from this picture to reveal

the "weather vane character" of the manner in which societies create helplessness and dependency, it would yield a more productive analysis. For instance, rather than assume that disabled people are the most vulnerable among us, why not consider the mechanisms that a society uses to make disabled people economically vulnerable, powerless, and isolated, and consider what the use of those mechanisms says about a society. Gilman (1985) does draw a distinction, parenthetically, between two types of vulnerability when he comments that medicine's "peculiar power lies not only in its status as science but in the overt helplessness of the individual in the face of illness (or in the face of being labelled ill)" (28).

Two other works take a somewhat different approach to centering disability perspectives. Radford (1994), in "Intellectual Disability and the Heritage of Modernity," explains that "modernity is a lens through which we can see that our culture has not only marginalized people with an intellectual disability, *it has also marginalized the study of intellectual disability as a phenomenon*" (22; Radford's emphasis). He explains the ways that the university and the broader forces of modernity in the nineteenth and twentieth centuries created the category of "mental deficiency" and the asylums in which people so identified were housed. He is more successful in explaining how the lens of modernity shapes understanding of disability than he is in demonstrating how a disability perspective might enrich our understanding of modernism. Morris (1991), in *The Culture of Pain,* comes a bit closer when he traces the medical establishment's claim to the territory of understanding and responding to human pain. "The medicalization of pain is indeed so characteristic of our time that historians seeking a date to mark the advent of modernism might do far worse than select 1899, when salicylic acid was first commercially developed into . . . aspirin" (59–60). Although Radner is more aware of the meaning of these ideas for the social situation of disabled people than either Morris, or McCagg and Siegelbaum, Morris recognizes how the medicalization of pain, and by inference I would add conditions involving pain, have shaped modernism. Although I don't think it is useful to equate disability with pain or with illness because these connections often have little validity in either a medical or social sense, I include these examples here because I think Morris has been so successful at centering pain and interpreting it as a cultural phenomenon. He, and Zborowski (1960) and others before him, have taken something usually thought to be a distinctly biological event—pain—and demonstrated how it can be better understood employing the tools of literary criticism, historical analysis, anthropological investigation, or philosophical inquiry. A similar analysis of disability might begin with Morris's statement that if a pill were invented "guaranteeing life-time immunity from pain, we would at once have to set about reinventing what it means to be human" (20).

Together, these three essays point toward formulations that center disability perspectives in a comprehensive way and enrich understanding of both disability and, in this example, modernity.

3. Although traditionally the study of disability has been housed predominantly in the applied fields, the vast majority of work that explains and elaborates on the social-political paradigms is not found in that knowledge base. Therefore, for a number of reasons, the proposed comprehensive disability studies epistemology should be grounded in the humanities and social sciences, and reflect the interdisciplinary nature of the field.

There are at least three benefits of such a formulation. One is that at this juncture it is important to distinguish between disability studies per se and the typical study of disability found in the applied fields. The latter group, aimed at intervention, remediation, care, and cure, dominates thinking about disability and interferes with an understanding of social and political phenomena.

A second benefit is that important disability-related practices taught in the applied fields are not grounded in a coherent theoretical rationale (Linton 1994). For instance, current debates over separate (special education) versus integrated (inclusive) education are based more on predicted outcomes or on pragmatic considerations than they are on legal, moral, historical, or psychological theory. Skrtic (1992) comments that the debates over different models of integrating education "are forms of *naive pragmatism,* a mode of analysis and problem resolution that is premised on an unreflective acceptance of the assumptions that lie behind social practices"(205; Skrtic's emphasis). Separate education systems are based on the notion that there is a logical divide between disabled and nondisabled people, and that each group's educational needs follow from their diagnosis as nondisabled or disabled. The act of dividing in two the entire group of school-age children and segregating one set from the other is rarely argued on theoretical grounds and must be justified as an expedient response to a difficult situation.

Consider a related example. Eve Kosofsky Sedgwick's (1990) stated aim in *Epistemology of the Closet* was not to argue a particular side in the debates over homosexual and heterosexual definitional issues but to direct attention to the absence of a theoretical rationale for the creation of the binary categories homosexual and heterosexual. "The purpose of this book is not to adjudicate between the two poles of either of these contradictions, for, if its [the book's] argument is right, no epistemological grounding now exists from which to do so" (2). Similarly, disability studies needs to build the epistemology of our closets, our institutions, sheltered workshops, and "special" schools, and it must critique weak arguments for a bifurcated society. I recognize, and have stated in a number of ways here, that disabled people are emphasizing the distinction between nondisabled and disabled people for the purpose of unifying a previously fragmented group and identifying phenomena largely hidden by that fragmentation. Marking the border is a strategic endeavor not to separate the two groups further but to illuminate the lines that currently divide them.

A third benefit of emphasizing the liberal arts in formulating disability studies epistemology is that with increased integration of disabled people in society and wider recognition of disability rights issues, the types of blatant control that existed in an era of institutionalization have been replaced by subtler forms of oppression and alienation. The examination of "the everyday habits and cultural meanings of which people are for the most part unaware" (Young 1990, 124) could be a strong suit of courses in the humanities. Although the social sciences and the applied fields have set the terms for the discourse of deviance, pathology, and normalcy, and have done little to challenge those constructs, representations of disability appearing throughout the humanities deepen the divide between disabled and nondisabled people and are similarly ignored.

Ultimately, disability studies can be most effective as an interdisciplinary field that can bring multiple perspectives to bear on the phenomenon of disability and can present disability as an organizing principle used to formulate questions, hypotheses, and a coherent knowledge base. As I noted in the introduction when cataloguing the limitations of my own field of psychology as a base from which to generate scholarship on disability, the questions that need to be addressed require new paradigms and a reading across the disciplines to render a more accurate, cohesive, and comprehensive picture of disability.

4. A fourth domain—related to the third—that disability studies scholars have attended to is the vast realm of meaning-making that occurs in metaphoric and symbolic uses of disability. These devices need to be analyzed in an array of cultural products to understand their meanings and functions, and to subvert their power. An impressive and rapidly growing body of work has taken on this task, and it is among the most useful and potent tools we can use to unveil attitudes toward disability (Thomson 1997; Davis 1995).

Metaphors related to disability are powerful tools of persuasion. "[P]erhaps the only defense against being victimized by metaphor is sophistication" (Kliebard 1992, 210). Susan Sontag (1978) raised our level of sophistication in *Illness as Metaphor*, in which she attempted to separate the essential from the nonessential aspects of illness, and, by inference, disability. Her purpose is to liberate our thinking from the "punitive or sentimental fantasies concocted about illness" (3). Kriegel (1982), in a discussion of Sontag's work, notes that "disease has become so all-embracing a metaphor that its actual physical consequences have been swallowed up by the welter of moralistic judgments it calls forth" (17). Neither Sontag nor Kriegel, however, has sited these interpretations in the context of disability politics, a natural avenue for an exploration of the consequences of these metaphors for the lived experience of people so labeled. Similarly, Thomson (1994) notes in an article on feminist disability studies that in two books that contribute to an understanding of that domain, although not described by the authors as disability studies, Herndl's (1993) *Invalid Women* and Huet's (1993) *Monstrous Imagination,* "disability itself is not politicized in either book" (589). Yet Herndl, for instance, "examines the dialectical relationship between the fact of invalidism and the figure of the invalid [so] freighted with cultural meaning" and, in doing so, "provides the source for a cultural figure that at once embodies . . . the contradictory discourses of womanhood in nineteenth century America" (590). In other words, a number of authors engage in an incomplete version of disability studies, one devoid of a social and political analysis of disability.

The metaphors that allude to disability or invoke disability imagery are everywhere, and the ideas they are based on are accepted so casually that we will have a hard time dissuading people from using them. An example, so subtle and so unexpected that it may slip unchecked into your thinking, comes from *Transforming Knowledge,* Elizabeth Kamarck Minnich's (1990) excellent book on curriculum transformation. It is a passage from Anna Julia Cooper's

Voice from the South, written more than one hundred years ago, in 1892:

> It is not the intelligent woman vs. the ignorant woman nor the white woman vs. the black, the brown, and the red, it is not even the cause of woman vs. man. Nay, 'tis woman's strongest vindication for speaking that *the world needs to hear her voice.* . . . The world has had to limp along with the wobbling gait and the one-sided hesitancy of a man with one eye. Suddenly the bandage is removed from the other eye and the whole body is filled with light. It sees a circle where before it saw a segment. The darkened eye restored, every member rejoices with it. (Frontispiece; emphasis in original)

This is certainly a vivid passage. Yet, its utility in this context rests on the belief that someone with the use of one eye perceives only a segment of the world, is unsteady, hesitant, and functions in a body filled with darkness. The parallels drawn between silenced women and disabled man, and then between women given a voice and a man who is "cured" appear to be as meaningful today as they were in 1892. The dilemma now for those who advocate curricular transformation, is to find ways not only to give voice to silenced women but to give voice to people with impaired vision. The benefit would be the increased ability to see this man, and other "uncured" human beings, as whole, purposeful, sentient people. If he remains a metaphor, his experience is defined only by implied comparison to unsteadiness, darkness, limited vision, sadness, ineptness, the absence of light and enlightenment, and any number of other substitutions for the real experience of women and men with disabilities.[2]

What is foregrounded here is assumed to be charged and redolent with meaning, the background neutral, useful as a device to emphasize the point. But I see the background as problematic, meaningful in its own right. It screams to be looked at. The representation reduces the man with a disability to a metaphor for inadequacy and this has consequences for disabled people. And because we are seeing with only a portion of our population, it has consequences for everyone.

Courses in literature, literary criticism, rhetoric, or philosophy can investigate these metaphors and other devices that seem appealing because they effectively evoke feelings or images that many are thought to share. Yet, these figures of speech further objectify and alienate people with disabilities and perpetuate inaccurate information about disabled people's experience. Consider, for instance, the accuracy of the ideas perpetuated in the passage above. There is probably no reason that a one-eyed person would see only part of a circle, and no reason to believe that someone with partial sight would, necessarily, stumble. Depth perception is often affected by sight in one eye, but people usually learn to accommodate to that change and adjust the way they walk.

Critical analysis is also needed of characters with disabilities and the functions they serve in fiction, film, and drama. For instance, renditions of characters such as Richard the Third, Laura Wingfield, Lord Chatterly, or Dr. Strangelove have a powerful impact on our thinking about disability. A number of authors working in this area have done exciting research. Norden's (1994) comprehensive study, *The Cinema of Isolation: A History of Physical Disability in the Movies,* examines characters with disabilities, disability-related themes and images that function as plot devices or metaphors, as well as formal mechanisms such as camera angles, framing, and editing to demonstrate how "most movies have tended to isolate disabled characters from their able-bodied peers as well as from each other" (1). Thomson's (1990) article on the representation of disability as stigma in the novels of Toni Morrison prompted one of my students to comment: "I've read all the novels by Morrison that she mentions and I must now go back and read them all again." The student, who is a graduate student in a rehabilitation program and works with people with disabilities, had not really noticed the disabled characters and had certainly missed the pattern that Thomson traces of Morrison's nonstereotypical depiction of disabled characters as vibrant, purposeful, and often strong women. Thomson finds that in Morrison's hands, "physically disabled or anomalous black women triumph" and the novels "repudiate stigmatization itself" (240). Other contributions include Kriegel's (1969) "Uncle Tom and Tiny Tim: Some Reflections on the Cripple as Negro"; Kent's (1988) essay "In Search of a Heroine: Images of Women with Disabilities in Fiction and Drama"; and Zola's (1987) "The Portrayal of Disability in the Crime Mystery Genre."

It is important now to move toward the establishment of a cohesive theoretical framework for this material. Further, we need to trace patterns in the use of metaphors and in symbolic uses of disability to determine where and how they emerge, and how they function in various genres, cultures, and historical periods. Gender, race, and class analyses of these representations should be integral to this endeavor.

The above four areas are what seem to me to be most pressing as we forge an epistemology of relevance to the broader academic community. The first, creating theories that conceptualize disabled and nondisabled people as integral, complementary parts of a whole universe, should consider the historical and cross-cultural research on practices that divide communities along disability lines, as well as those that unite people and promote equity. Those practices are gender-, class-, and race-specific, and theory should not be naive with respect to the complexity of these interactions. The second, developing a cohesive knowledge base that positions disability as the central vector of analysis, is a creative enterprise that should see no boundaries to the production of the idea of "disability." The third, grounding disability in the humanities and social sciences and rendering an interdisciplinary field, is essential to address the unanswered questions or, even more fundamentally, to formulate questions unimaginable from our present constricted knowledge base. The last enterprise is to mine the canons for the malignant, unsavory, or simply reductive representations of disability that insinuate themselves into our thinking. Metaphor is not merely an "ornament to speech and writing irrelevant to the task of clarifying and conveying meaning," it is a "fundamental vehicle of human thought" (Kliebard 1992, 206) and, as such, has a profound impact on thinking about people with disabilities. We should also attempt to dissuade authors from utilizing disability in this way in future writing—possibly by demonstrating how these metaphors are often used reflexively to trigger a reaction rather than to illustrate or explain an idea.

Whatever renovations are performed on the curriculum to develop disability studies and integrate it into the curriculum, these actions are not taking place in isolation. The quotations that appear at the opening of chapter 1 demonstrate my belief in the dynamic interaction between the civic and pedagogic cultures. Kliebard's belief that the curriculum is a manifest expression of the cultural values is coupled with Minnich's statement that educational institutions are the shapers and guardians of cultural memory and hence of cultural meanings. As currently rendered, the knowledge we generate in the academy and disseminate to students perpetuates a society in which disabled people are often cast as other, marginalized, and denied civil rights and economic opportunity; relegated to segregated and inferior education; and restricted in their opportunities for pleasure, social and sexual interaction, parenting, marriage, religious expression, and freedom of movement.

As the inquiry moves further into the academy, there is a danger that it may lose some of its potential to change academic and civic practices. Shumway and Messer-Davidow (1991) raise a similar concern about separating feminist inquiry and activism. In their article on disciplinarity they ask: "If the movement is no longer the context for knowledge-production, many now wonder, will feminism be able to remain a transformational project?" (216). Disability studies should stay tethered to the disability rights movement from which it was born and should remain committed to serving not only knowledge production but civil rights, justice, and equity.

NOTES

1. Some of the material from this passage originally appeared in Linton, Mello, and O'Neill (1994). John O'Neill and Susan Mello contributed a great deal to this interpretation.
2. Elizabeth Minnich and I have been engaged in an ongoing dialogue about some of the issues I raise in this analysis. It has been wonderful to "think out loud" with her, and her insights have enriched my thinking on this passage.

6

DISABILITY STUDIES/
NOT DISABILITY STUDIES

The border between what is considered disability studies and what is not is fixed at different points by different authors and researchers. Although it is unlikely that anyone would suggest that there be an absolute boundary, efforts to circumscribe the domain and to anticipate the consequences of limitless permeability across the borders are worthwhile. In this chapter, I am concerned with providing a coherent rationale for marking a border, setting off disability studies as a socio-political-cultural examination of disability from the interventionist approaches that characterize the dominant traditions in the study of disability.

The field of disability studies arose, in part, as counterpoint to the medicalized perspectives on disability emanating from the applied fields, and in response to the marginalization and distortions apparent across the curriculum. In one sense, the development of disability studies is a remedial endeavor, redressing the sins of omission and commission in the canon. Yet, in a significant way, disability studies moves beyond the corrective. It is the socio-political-cultural model of disability incarnate. It provides an epistemological basis for inquiries and actions that could not have been imagined from the restrictive thresholds of the traditional curriculum.

It is timely to mark this border because the name "Disability Studies" has begun to crop up around the United States and Great Britain to describe graduate and undergraduate programs in everything from the training of health care workers and occupational therapists to courses in literary criticism examining representation and metaphor. The health and occupational therapy programs' appropriation of "Disability Studies" compromises the integrity of a field designed to explicate disability as a social, political, and cultural phenomenon. In this chapter, I am labeling those applied approaches the "Not Disability Studies." For reasons to be described here, I name them as such not to denigrate their function but to explain how the appropriation of the term compromises the validity and utility of a separate liberal arts–based inquiry.

FAULTS AND FAULT LINES

In considering here how we might effectively and validly delineate disability studies, I'd like to begin by outlining the limitations or problems in the dominant or traditional curriculum's presentation of disability. Following is a list of the faults and fault lines, that is, the more clearly observable misrepresentations, as well as the covert problems in the academic curriculum that determine how disability is studied. They are presented as motivating forces for the establishment of a discrete field of disability studies, grounded in the liberal arts and set apart from the applied fields. Each is then examined to determine how best to redress it through the development of disability studies.

1. The current presentation of disability, predominantly in rehabilitation and in special education, individualizes disability—the curriculum fosters the idea that disability is the individual's or at most the family's problem. Further, the curriculum treats disability as an isolable phenomenon, and ideas about it relate only to it and to people who have particular conditions.

2. The construction of disability as, perforce, a problem interferes with its being viewed as an issue, an idea, a metaphor, a phenomenon, a culture, and a construction.

3. The absence of subjectivity and agency of disabled people is evident in a review of standard curricula in history, psychology, women's studies, literature, philosophy, anthropology, and on and on. Moreover, the problem is compounded by the absence of disabled people's perspectives in the general culture.

4. The objectification of disabled people in scholarship, which in part is a consequence of the absence of subjectivity and the active voice of disabled researchers, but is also made possible by the dominance of empiricism in the study of disability; the large number of stereotypes and simplified versions of disabled people's experience presented across the disciplines; the absence of critical analysis; the pathologizing of experience; and the use of diagnostic categories or other means of labeling.

5. Across the curriculum in the social sciences and in the applied fields, essentialist and deterministic explanations of disability abound.

6. As a result of the medicalization of disability in the traditional canon, there occurs a pathologizing of difference; the individ-

ualization of disability (see item 1, above); a loss of self-definition and self-determination; and a forced assignment of the roles of patient, client, and consumer. Related to this is the conflation of impairment and disability—lack of recognition that impairment and disability should be addressed predominantly in separate realms of discourse.

7. An overemphasis on intervention at the individual level, what Trickett, Watts, and Birman (1994) have spoken of as "person-fixing rather than context-changing" (18).

8. The preponderance of information on disability in the curricula of the applied fields effectively sequesters the study of disability in those fields, which deal with narrow bands of content and bring to bear a restricted range of methodology on their subjects.

9. Within the applied fields, there is inadequate attention to the interventions and to the medical and educational solutions that the disabled community has asked for.

10. The marginalization of the study of disability in the humanities and in the liberal arts in general.

11. Insufficient attention to disabled people as minority group and the cultural, political, and intellectual meanings of that status. Further, diversity initiatives and multicultural curriculum endeavors have, for the most part, ignored disability as a category of analysis.

12. And last, the curriculum is missing what I call an epistemology of inclusion. There does not exist a broad-based body of knowledge, an intellectual rationale for the incorporation of disabled people as full and equal members of society.

WHAT IS NEEDED

Given these problems, what is the most logical organization of the study of disability in the academy?

There should be a well-developed, interdisciplinary field of inquiry, grounded in the liberal arts and called disability studies, designed to study disability as a social, political, and cultural phenomenon.

Separate from an established disability studies, the applied fields should develop more valid and useful approaches to the presence of impairment in the population and disability in society, and respond to disabled people in a less deterministic and more integrated way than heretofore. Although their focus is on individual interventions, research and curricula should examine carefully the contextual variables that shape experience. Arokiasamy (1993) states that "the ultimate purpose of rehabilitation is the achievement of individual autonomy by the client . . . [and] in its pursuit of this purpose, rehabilitation should use a holistic approach to treatment . . . including the social, economic, political, cultural, and legal contexts in which people with disabilities find themselves" (81).

These revised applied approaches should be informed by the intellectual traditions inherent in disability studies and by the political commitments adhered to by the disability rights movement. Teaching in the applied fields should support inclusion, self-determination, and self-definition. Based on those tenets and informed by current research in education that supports inclusion, the programs should be revised so as to prepare professionals to work in integrated settings. I advocate the reconfiguring of special education and rehabilitation, which have traditionally overdetermined disability as an explanatory variable and which prepare people to work in segregated settings, exclusively with disabled people. However, no matter which revisions are made, the curriculum and body of research that supports intervention should remain in the category "Not Disability Studies." For reasons elaborated below, the maintenance of two separate domains has both intellectual and political significance.

RATIONALE

Let's return now to the list of problems with the traditional curriculum and consider the validity and utility of differentiating between disability studies and "not disability studies." Obviously, the applied approaches need a new name or multiple names. I am naming the not disability studies as the null hypothesis, not because it is devoid of substance but because it remains not fully articulated as a distinct field. Special education, rehabilitation, and other disability-related fields were and remain more clearly a reaction to social need than fields determined by a set of principles and ideas. Although social need is a reasonable basis for developing curricula, the perpetuation of these fields needs to be reevaluated in light of current research and social imperatives. Arokiasamy (1993), writing on the need for a theoretical basis for rehabilitation, notes that "rehabilitation as a profession and as a specific field . . . emerged largely out of legislative mandate . . . and in response to a series of practical needs . . . [which] has contributed to making rehabilitation a pragmatic, technique-driven profession without a sound theoretical base" (77). The medicalized fields, such as rehabilitation and even special education, which adopt the organization of knowledge used in medicine, have historically presumed dominion over all knowledge on disability. Therefore, for the purposes of this book, it is useful to center the disability studies model, from which standpoint the remaining study of disability is peripheral.

Recall that problem 1 is the *individualization of disability.* Maintaining the distinction between disability studies and applied approaches underscores that individual responses are appropriate for impairment but are misdirected for disability. The individualization of disability, although logical in the applied fields, has spilled over into all other curricula on disability.

Recall, also, problem 2, *disability as a problem.* People with disabilities have problems, and those may be addressed by individual interventions, but maintaining a separate liberal arts–based

137

disability studies would reinforce the idea that society creates many of the problems disabled people experience, and society has a responsibility to address them.

There are, of course, problems that are a direct result of impairment; pain, suffering, frustrations, and anxiety often accompany impairment, and no amount of social change or theory will take those away. Even though pain and even less extreme kinds of discomfort are mediated by social and political contingencies, they remain intensely personal experiences. I believe that discourse on the social, cultural, and political meaning of disability can and should take on these issues, which disability studies has not yet done successfully. Paul Longmore, in a personal conversation in 1996, described this gap in the literature as "the need to theorize about impairment." It is incumbent upon disability studies theorists to articulate these elements of experience because they are relevant to many areas of inquiry, from literary criticism to anthropology, from clinical psychology to cultural studies.

Disability studies theorists do need to grapple more directly with "impairment" and recognize that it is as nuanced and complex a construct as "disability." There has been much discussion about this, but it still remains unarticulated in theory.[1] We have been hesitant to go in a particular direction in the development of theory—that is, toward the issue of impairment itself. As we talk about it among ourselves, we've acknowledged that we have been reluctant to theorize about the actual pain and limitations that we experience. It may be the manifestation in theory of a personal denial of the impact and consequences of impairment. Yet it may also be the tremendous difficulty in articulating impairment in ways that do not essentialize disability or reduce it to an individual problem. I think we recognize that outside critics would be willing to latch onto ideas about impairment, and that would deflect attention from the more socially demanding issues such as civil rights or oppression.

We can look to writing in related domains for information on how to do this. Morris (1991), in *The Culture of Pain*, has done some interesting work theorizing about pain, something that is usually thought of as a distinctly biological event. He comments that "traditional Western medicine—by which I mean not so much individual doctors and researchers as an entire scientific-medical worldview that permeates our culture—has consistently led us to misinterpret pain as no more than a sensation, a symptom, a problem in biochemistry" (5). He closes his introduction by promising to elaborate on the meanings accorded to pain: "Pain on this new ground will . . . [be understood] . . . as an experience that also engages the deepest and most personal levels of the complex cultural and biological process we call living" (7). Morris's work is not a simple mind-over-matter orientation to pain, nor is it a palliative for people who experience pain to help them find meaning in their suffering; it is an entreaty to those too willing to be reductive in thinking about pain. He also makes a case for reconsideration of Western medicine's domination over the meanings accorded to pain, a point that disability studies scholars make repeatedly about medicine's claimed authority on disability and on impairment. In reducing pain or impairment to something that needs to be "fixed" and medicine as the remedy to that stated problem, medicine succeeds in cornering the market on knowledge about these phenomena.

Although I have raised the issue of impairment apropos of "problems," the explication of impairment should in no way be confined to experience that has a negative valence. A phenomenological approach to the study of impairment will yield the rich array of descriptions of experience that one is likely to overhear in the corridors at a Society for Disability Studies conference, or the back rooms of an independent living center: the insiders' experience of body, and of sensory, emotional, and cognitive functioning that is expressed most openly within disability circles.

One research domain that is yet to be fully explored from the perspective of disabled people is the kinesthetic, proprioceptive, sensory, and cognitive experiences of people with an array of disabilities. For instance, because I use a wheelchair, I utilize my upper body for mobility and rock back and forth as I propel myself forward. My height when I am vertical differs from my measured height horizontally, and my impairment influences my height relative to objects in the world and to other people. Each of these experiences has an impact on my sense of my body in space and affects the information I am exposed to and the way I process sensory information.

Given that my experience or the experience of someone who is blind or deaf, or of someone who has mental retardation has been underrepresented across the disciplines, we are missing the constructs and theoretical material needed to articulate the ways impairment shapes disabled people's version of the world. Even as I write this, I am struggling to find the words to describe these phenomena adequately. It is particularly difficult to find language to describe my experience that is not relational, meaning descriptions that do not measure my movements in relation to nondisabled norms. The fact that impairment has almost always been studied from a deficit model means that we are deficient in language to describe it any other way than as a "problem."

The work of Oliver Sacks comes to mind as someone who has attempted to reframe the discourse on impairment. Unfortunately, there is a clinical overlay to his material and an assumption of a doctor-patient configuration that compromise his project. Particularly in the theatrical presentation of his work in *The Man Who*, in which "doctors" costumed in white lab coats interview "patients," the disabled persons' experience is not depathologized; rather, their quirks are turned into objects of aesthetic interest, and the doctor's competence in diagnosis and interpretation is valorized. Sacks and others, such as Thomas Szasz and R. D. Laing, do attempt to dissociate "disability" from "problem," but to the extent that their work fails to account for the authors' relative power and for their claimed authority for their subjects' experience, it is an incomplete endeavor contributing more to the appropriation of disabled people's experience than to its elucidation. Further, Sacks's work, although hailed as a literary achievement, fails as a disability studies project because it does not contribute to the self-determination or self-definition of disabled people, and does not explicate a socio-political-cultural understanding of disability. As Tom Shakespeare (1996) said, in a review of *An Anthropologist on Mars,* "Oliver Sacks, the man who mistook his patients for a literary career, violates every existing principle of disability equality. . . . He describes himself as 'making house calls at the far border of experience', but he is more like a colonialist than a general practitioner" (139). Given these criticisms, it is important to consider whether, in fact, Sacks's essays do succeed as literary works in that they are unlikely to stimulate the readership to view disabled people in their complexity, as sentient, purposeful people. All of this is to say, just because material on disability emerges in the liberal arts, it is not necessarily disability studies if it does not challenge the notions that disability is an individual condition and a problem needing medical solutions.

Problem 3 is the *absence of subjectivity in scholarship.* The voice of disabled people should be present in both disability studies and applied approaches to disabled people, but the voice should take different form in each. The influence and direction of disabled people should permeate the applied fields. If rehabilitation professionals really believe in self-determination for disabled people, they should practice what they teach by adhering to an active affirmative action program in their own departments; by adopting the books and essays of disabled people into their curricula; and by demanding that disabled people have an active voice in conference planning and on the platform at conferences. In the liberal arts, the active voice, the creative voice, the narrative, can be articulated in the humanities, and in qualitative and interpretative research in the social sciences.

Women's studies has demonstrated the scholarly potential of personal narratives by mapping the way to interpret the personal as the political and as the scholarly. Feminist scholarship has also turned the entire academic curriculum inside out to reveal the epistemological consequences of the androcentric biases in the knowledge base. Disability studies scholars are also explicating the political and scholarly antecedents and consequences of personal experience. Now scholars of all stripes must recognize their moral and intellectual obligation to evaluate the gaps and faults in the knowledge base they disseminate to students that result from the missing voices of disabled people.

Problem 4, *the objectification of disabled people,* can be redressed by developing scholarship from the position of the disabled subject; by developing alternative methodologies to the empiricist approaches that have dominated the study of disability; by developing the active voice in the humanities; and by breaking down stereotypes through the analysis of metaphors, images, and all representations of disability in the academic and popular cultures. The overwhelming majority of scholarship on disability either utilizes or implies the third-person plural: "they" do this, "they" are like that, "they" need such and such. This contributes to the objectification of disabled people and contributes to the experience of alienation disabled people so often report.

Problem 5 is *essentialist and deterministic explanations.* As with much of the transformative scholarship on race and gender, disability studies serves a remedial function, necessary to correct omissions, inaccuracies, and faulty logic. Two particularly pernicious ideas that need to be vigorously contested are *determinist arguments* that explain human behavior and achievement in terms of biology and those that explain achievement in terms of individual psychological makeup.

Feminist studies, disability studies, and African American studies, among others, challenge the notion that biology is destiny. Each elaborates on the mutability of human behavior to counteract essentialist arguments and to demonstrate that there are few human practices that are inevitable. Specifically, disability studies challenges the assumption that the social and economic status and assigned roles of people with disabilities are a consequence of disabled people's "natural" inferiority. However, "unlike other minorities, . . . disabled men and women have not yet been able to refute implicit or direct accusations of biological inferiority that have often been invoked to rationalize the oppression of groups whose appearance differs from the standards of the dominant majority" (Hahn 1988, 26).

Yet, even when biological arguments for difference in social position are discredited, there remains the persistent belief that the cause of social disadvantage is within individuals and that change is dependent on personal transformation. Psychological explanations of the behavior and social position of members of minority groups have a prominent place in traditional curricula. For instance, the meaning most often accorded disability is that it is a personal condition rather than a social issue, an individual plight rather than a political one. When individuals with disabilities fail in education, employment, or love, the failure is attributed either to the disability, itself considered an obstacle to achievement, or to the individual's psychological weaknesses or lack of resiliency, the inability to "overcome" misfortune.

These explanations foreground the individual and give little consideration to the barriers, discrimination, negative imagery, and lack of opportunity that shape experience. Within this framework, efforts aimed at helping the individual cope with and adjust to personal tragedies seem most logical. To further this myopic view of the experience of disability, news stories about disability are invariably human interest tales of individual accomplishment, dense in the rhetoric of "overcoming," the narrative of personal triumph over adversity.

Education, clinical psychology, and other social sciences have been particularly influential in creating these deterministic narratives. These fields conceptualize disability as deviance from the norm, as pathological condition, and as deficit, and concentrate their efforts on the measurement of individual deviance, pathology, and deficits. This structure posits an ideal standard of physical, psychological, and sensory functioning from which any disability is considered a deviation. This is remarkably similar to the traditional evaluation of women, described by Carol Tavris (1992) in *The Mismeasure of Woman*. She tells of the way research has often measured women against some idealized male norm, attempting to explain women's behavioral differences in terms of perceived biological or psychological differences rather than differences in power and circumstance. Thomson (1990), in discussing the position of people with disabilities in society, reminds us of the power differential between nondisabled and disabled people, reinforced because "the dominant group defines itself as normative" (239). Analyses such as these are essential to help focus attention on the processes that center and privilege certain people and characteristics.

Scholarship that relies on individual deterministic explanations of social phenomena is also used to explain racism, sexism, and ableism. Adolph Reed (1995) notes that the development of psychological explanations of racism came about in the late 1930s when an "elite commitment to scientific racism, rooted in biologistic defenses of inequality, was eroding." Reed believes that Gunnar Myrdal's (1944) *An American Dilemma: The Negro Problem and Modern Democracy* ushered in a period of describing "racism in individual, psychological terms rather than in relation to state

DISABILITY STUDIES/NOT DISABILITY STUDIES

action." Myrdal's framework "reduced racism to the level of *beliefs* that whites held about blacks" (506; Reed's emphasis). A similarly individualistic explanation pervades the vast literature on attitudes toward disability that examines personality variables as they relate to nondisabled peoples' acceptance or rejection of disabled people as friends, classmates, or lovers.

The introduction of the social explanations found in the disability studies literature broadens the investigation of ableism to include social conditions that mediate responses to disability. The conditions include the economic and social structures that affect the relative position of and interactions between disabled and nondisabled people. The conditions also include the nature and quality of representations of disability in all curriculum domains and in cultural products. Of course, the degrees of integration in living arrangements, educational institutions, and cultural and social environments are essential components of this analysis, as are the political climate and legislative safeguards that influence social interactions.

Therefore, to counteract essentializing and deterministic narratives of disability, the field of disability studies should focus on social, political, and cultural analyses. This shift affords a more comprehensive view of society and human experience, and the attribution of significance to human variation. These types of analysis challenge the biological as well as the individual and psychological explanations of human experience, achievement, and behavior.

Other problems listed include the *medicalization of disability* (6), *overemphasis on intervention* (7), and *the disproportionate amount of information on disability in the applied fields* (8). All of these can be helped by delineating between disability studies and the applied approaches. Because there has been so much emphasis on the applied approaches, with their medicalized version of disability, these ideas tend to spill over into all other inquiry into disability. In housing the social, political, and cultural inquiry into disability in a separate liberal arts–based domain—disability studies—and making the field robust, the medicalized paradigms can be used only where appropriate, and the political, social, and cultural paradigms can be understood as valid organizing tools for knowledge on disability.

Within the applied fields, there is *inadequate response to the educational and medical interventions the disability community deems important* (problem 9). I am advocating a liberal arts–based disability studies, but the applied fields would benefit from an infusion of disability studies scholarship and disability rights perspectives.

To begin, it is essential that leadership and control of disability-related services be in the hands of disabled people. In both the academic and community response to the educational and health care needs of disabled people, disabled people are relegated to the patient, student, or client role, and rarely get to be the professor, the teacher, the clinician, or clinic director. Further, the model of inclusion currently being applied in a number of elementary and secondary educational settings, where full integration of disabled and nondisabled children is taking place, should be applied to health care services as well, so that disabled people are not restricted to rehabilitation facilities and other specialized services for their health care needs.

The leadership of disabled people in the applied fields can take many forms, as can their influence on practices. Clearly, professors and professionals with disabilities would be extremely important. Collaborative projects with community organizations would be another form. In addition, students should learn about the history of their practice, and about the social and political issues that frame their work. Provision of this type of contextual material would help students evaluate the impact of the dominance of the medical profession, almost exclusively nondisabled, on types of interventions designed for disabled people. The issues of control, self-determination, and self-definition can be discussed within such a framework.

Poetry, film, and other creative products can also be used to introduce disability perspectives into the applied fields. In a recent *Disability Studies Quarterly* a book on African-American perspectives on health, illness, aging, and loss was reviewed. It is an anthology of poetry and prose to be used by those entering the medical profession, mostly non–African Americans, to provide insight into customs, beliefs, and cultural practices valued by African Americans. Other voices of disabled people can be brought into professional programs in the applied fields through such vehicles. Courses in disability studies should be offered in the professional programs, in part as a means to bring the active voice of disabled people into the academic curriculum. For instance, I teach a course in a rehab program; officially titled "Social and Psychological Aspects of Disability," it actually is a basic liberal arts survey course in disability studies. We read literary criticism, view films, discuss current issues in the disability rights movement, read anthropological and historical materials, and review psychological theory, with a disability reading of that theory. Because students don't obtain a liberal arts education in disability nor a political education in disability anywhere else in their education, I think it is critical to provide that within the professional programs. It is hoped that each of these strategies will help future practitioners remain alert to the rights of disabled people, and alert to disabled people's authority and knowledge. It is particularly important for disabled students in these programs to be exposed to disability history and culture.

The liberal arts, particularly the humanities, have barely noticed disability (problem 10) beyond the models that they accept uncritically, handed down from the sciences and medicine. The tools of inquiry in the humanities have, until recently, rarely been applied to understanding disability as phenomenon. A simple test reveals the obscurity of disability; a search of a data base in history, literature, or philosophy using the descriptors *disability, disabled,* or *disability studies* is unavailing. Yet if you search your internal data base (inside your head), you are likely to recognize the pervasiveness of disability in regard to historical figures, consequences of war, literary representation, metaphor, ethical issues, symbolism, subject matter in cultural products, and any number of other themes, ideas, or concrete events where human beings are involved. Even in the social sciences, the study of disability is cordoned off into courses such as the sociology of deviance, abnormal psychology, and medical anthropology, which assume the logic of the medical view of disability as deficit, as pathology, and as problem.

Problem 11: *Insufficient attention is given to the minority-group status of disabled people, and the cultural, social and political meanings of that status throughout the curriculum.* Advocates in the applied fields have often worked toward political change for disabled people, and it is hoped they always will, but their actions do not emanate from the knowledge base and approaches used in the applied fields; their actions stem from personal and moral commitments to improve the lives of disabled people. Arokiasamy (1993) writes that "the rehabilitation practitioner, neither by training nor job role, is suited for activism of such macro proportions" (84). He distinguishes between societal-level (macro) and individual-level advocacy; the latter, he believes, is best accomplished by teaching and encouraging self-advocacy in "clients." My purpose here is not to discourage political activism. Indeed, the more committed those in the applied fields are, the better. However, we need to recognize that these actions have no basis in the curriculum that students in the applied fields are exposed to.

In both the applied fields and in liberal arts–based disability studies courses, there are a number of places where ideas and information about disabled people's social and political status could be covered. In the applied fields, course material could cover the history and current status of practice, with particular attention to the relative power and privilege of health and education practitioners, even those who are disabled, compared with that of the disabled community they serve. Courses in disability studies would, of course, cover the political issues involved in the disability rights movement and the independent living movement, as well as the factors that impede political change.

Before turning to problem 12 and explaining how differentiating between disability studies and "not disability studies" can address it, a few other related issues should be kept in mind.

First, consider how the distinction among the terms *disability*, *handicap*, and *impairment* have benefited the development of scholarship on disability and have benefited disabled people. The differentiation has focused attention on the social and political contingencies that shape disabled peoples' lives. In developing curriculum, we should follow that same logic and utilize the term *disability studies* solely for investigations of disability as a social, cultural, and political phenomenon.

Similarly, deaf scholars have made the distinction between *Deaf*, to identify those who share a language and a culture, and *deaf*, to identify those with the audiological condition of not hearing, in order to focus attention on the cultural construction of deafness. As Padden and Humphries (1988) write, the "knowledge of Deaf people is not simply a camaraderie with others who have a similar physical condition, but is . . . historically created and actively transmitted across generations" (2). Yet the study of deafness in most institutions remains mired in a medicalized, interventionist discourse and the study of Deaf culture rarely appears in the liberal arts curriculum. A recent ad in the *New York Times* for an academic position listed an opening for a "Deaf Studies Instructor." On the next line it said, "Duties: Teaching American Sign Language and other human services courses. . . ." I am not arguing here for the elimination of human services courses, although I frequently, with little provocation, argue for a change in their form and ideological underpinnings; I am making a point about the use of the terms *disability studies* or *Deaf studies* to describe them. The adoption of the term *disability studies* by the applied fields as a hip way of labeling curriculum they've always taught does a disservice to scholars working to establish the validity and internal consistency of this field.

Looking at the history of women's studies, we can see similar struggles. The field early on differentiated between the meaning of *sex* and *gender*. Recognizing that gender is socially constructed does not preclude understanding or responding to sex as primarily a biological event. Similarly, creating the term *women's studies* to describe the meaning and function of gender in all its manifestations does not obviate the need for an academic response to *sex*. Therefore, just as gynecology can be thought of as an academic response to sex, rehabilitation can be thought of as an academic response to impairment, or audiology to deafness. And, in the same way that women's studies has influenced the training and delivery of service in gynecology, disability studies can and should influence the curriculum and practice in rehabilitation and special education, and Deaf studies can influence audiology.

A second point. Disabled people and their allies have fought to delineate disabled people as a minority group. The continuum approach—the idea that there should be no distinction made between disabled and nondisabled people—doesn't wash when you observe the specific treatment of disabled people in society. Therefore, articulating the ways that disabled people are a minority group is a strategic endeavor to focus on the social construction of disability and the treatment of the named minority group. There are also epistemological consequences of explaining the ways that disabled and nondisabled people are distinct groups. If, throughout the curriculum, disability were to be recognized as a minority-group status and as a marker of identity, it would have an impact on the entrenched view that disability is a problem, and an individual, medical problem. Further, the marked category would help organize knowledge on representations of the group and focus attention on the absence of voice from the perspective of members of the group. The move to secure the distinction between disability studies and the applied fields' response to disability is consonant with the distinction between disabled and nondisabled, and between disability and impairment. The need for a distinct field of disability studies is premised on the belief that disability has been socially constructed and that construction serves a variety of intellectual and social ends. The facets of that construction can be illuminated by alterations in the content of the curriculum in each field and by a shift in the placement of the study of disability within the curriculum.

A third rationale for delineating between disability studies and the applied fields is uncovered by tracing the history of women's studies and comparing it with the trajectory of disability studies. Although it is understandable that some of the early work in disability studies came from within the applied fields, where disability has traditionally been studied, it is time to separate the two areas and illuminate the boundaries between them. In the history of feminist inquiry, the "applied fields, most notably applied ethics were the first areas in which feminist work was published." There is a logic to that because "feminism is first and last, a political movement concerned with practical issues. At first, the more abstract areas of philosophy seemed distant from these concrete concerns." Feminists began to realize that they could address social problems not only through the applied fields when they saw "the problems produced by androcentrism in . . . the 'core' areas of epistemology" (Alcoff and Potter 1993, 2)—in other words, in the more abstract philosophical inquiries. I note this to point out an important distinction: the "applied fields" in feminism's history—

for example, applied ethics—are not focused on individual, biologically derived problems of women but on social and cultural ones, so applied ethics was a logical place to address the social "problems" that feminism was concerned with.

People concerned with the practical problems of ableism will have to work broadly across the disciplines to unearth how and where discrimination against and marginalization of disabled people can be studied. There are few tools available in the *medicalized* applied fields that can conduct such an inquiry, and the paltry representation of disability in the liberal arts have made such investigations difficult. Further, as Messer-Davidow (1991) notes, "[T]he *making* of social change does not exist as an academic inquiry." She goes on to say that it is more typical to "study *what* gets changed and *when* it gets changed, but not *how* it changes. . . . Studies that do focus on these processes often are regarded as 'popular' rather than scholarly and thus dismissed by the academy" (293).

A fourth issue before returning to the list of responses to problems in the traditional curriculum: A question that is heard in disability studies circles—and has been for years in women's studies, lesbian and gay studies, and so on—is, who should teach and write in the field? Whether disabled or nondisabled people create scholarship has particular consequences for the scholarship produced and for disabled people's lives. Both disabled and nondisabled people can perpetuate or work to ameliorate the objectification of disabled people, the lack of subjectivity, the absence of voice, and the absence of self-definition and self-determination. I don't assume that disabled people are exempt from the tendency to stereotype or objectify; after all, disabled people and nondisabled people have both been schooled in the same ableist discourse. Nondisabled people, though, have a particular responsibility to engage consciously and deliberately with these issues in their scholarship and teaching to avoid contributing to the problem. I think that it is incumbent on nondisabled scholars to pay particular attention to issues of their own identity, their own privilege as nondisabled people, and the relationship of these factors to their scholarship.

Analyses of the specifics of one's identity or status as it affects scholarship should not be thought of in reductive terms such as "identity politics" or the even more obfuscatory "politically correct." In any way that scholarship can be influenced by identity, social position, experience, sensory acuity, cognitive functioning, physical configuration and functioning, or other characteristics, scholars need to account for or control for that influence. In the same way that social scientists have always been taught to control for variables that might influence their research, all scholars should account for the influence related to experience and point of view as it directly relates to the research at hand. Further, as I mentioned earlier, the articulated or implied third-person "they," which is pervasive in scholarship on disability, increases the objectification of disabled people. That, along with the absence of subjectivity, has an impact on self-determination and self-definition—so critical to disabled people's lives.

Stating one's position relative to the subject matter is of theoretical importance and it is also of political importance. Stating that one identifies as disabled or nondisabled calls attention to the absent voice of disabled people in scholarship and illustrates that the reader may tend to make the assumption, although probably not consciously, that the writer is nondisabled. Feminist, African American, and lesbian and gay studies have followed this convention for a long time, marking the female, black, and lesbian and gay voice. It is interesting that recently the male, white, heterosexual identity is being marked more systematically and theorized, with essays on "whiteness" appearing with the most frequency. I am suggesting that nondisabled and disabled scholars working in disability studies follow that tradition and discuss their subject position and the consequences for their scholarship in similarly complex and meaningful ways.

Further, those writing in disability studies can challenge the minimal presence of disabled scholars in the institutions with which they are affiliated. They can examine in scholarship the history and consequences of discrimination in education and employment, the absence of affirmative action guidelines for disabled people, and the failure of institutions of higher education to evidence a commitment to disabled people and disability issues, other than that mandated by law. As scholars, we can use the tools of our trade toward shifting this trend. Further, both disabled and nondisabled scholars can review their commitments to the tenets of disability studies and to the disabled community by considering how they engage disabled people within and outside the academy in their work. As an example, Carol Gill, a disabled woman, a psychologist, and director of the Chicago Institute on Disability Research, shared with me notes she wrote for a paper presented at the 1996 Society for Disability Studies conference. She reported an incident that demonstrates the failure of commitment that some researchers evidence to the disabled community and to equity.

> A team of health professionals announce their commitment to participatory action research in developing an educational video on a disability topic. They characterize their project as "inclusive." . . . They say it is guided by our perspective. In fact, the only role given to people with disabilities is the opportunity to serve on a "consensus panel"—a kind of continuing focus group whose aim is to teach the researchers what they should cover in the video. Of course, people with disabilities also serve as the interview subjects in the film. For their efforts. the consensus panel members get snacks, no money. The interview subjects get $50 each. The health professionals are highly offended when I tell them this is not inclusion. They refuse to hire a professional with a disability to give substantive consulting services. They also refuse to share authorship with a disabled collaborator. Yet, they

hound me for weeks to serve on the consensus panel with the other "consumers."

In the paper, Gill cited three more incidences of disregard for the expertise and authority of disabled people.

Two years ago I was similarly confounded by the behavior of faculty members engaged in disability research. I learned that a group of faculty was organizing a major conference to present the university's work across a range of disciplines in disability research. The conference was being planned as a precursor to establishing an institute or center on disability research at the university, and therefore the nature of the conference and the choice of the personnel involved had significant long-term consequences. I began to ask questions about who was on the planning committee and learned that of the ten or so people, not one was a disabled person. The members had been meeting for some time and apparently no one had made an issue of this. A group of disabled people initiated a series of meetings with the steering committee and the president of the institution to protest the composition of the committee. A group of us—members of the faculty and staff already engaged in research on disability—were allowed to join the planning committee. We attended a number of long planning sessions, significantly shifted the focus of the conference, and, to my mind, improved its scope and vision considerably. We then received brief letters saying that the conference had been canceled indefinitely, and despite phone calls and letters to the organizers, we have never been given a satisfactory answer as to why it was canceled.

These examples are included to point out that disability studies is an intellectual as well as political endeavor and that these are reciprocal enterprises. Oliver (1992) has written about the need to change "the social relations of research production" (106). He sees it not simply as a matter of switching from positivist models of research to interpretive methods but, more significantly, as a need to understand the power relationships that "structure the social relations of research production" (110). Oliver's work points to the need to consider the contextual variables that shape what we study and how we study it.

Returning now to the last problem, problem 12: within the traditional curriculum, there is not a well-developed epistemological foundation for an inclusive society. What is needed is a broad-based liberal arts, interdisciplinary inquiry into the function and meaning of disability in all its manifestations. This inquiry should be similar in structure to women's studies and lesbian and gay studies, and as such would be informed by the political movements that generated the field, by cultural studies, and by the traditional disciplines. It should go beyond analyzing the exclusion of disabled people from society and of disability from the epistemological traditions in society to chart the people's and the subjects' place in the civic and academic cultures. That is disability studies.

NOTES

1. I have been informed in my thinking about this by conversations with Paul Longmore, David Mitchell, Harilyn Rousso, and Rosemarie Garland Thomson.

7

APPLICATIONS

Every year increasing numbers of students, both disabled and nondisabled, are entering college from primary and secondary schools where mainstreamed classrooms are common. Future incoming students will have been part of inclusive classrooms, where not only a few high-performing physically disabled children but a spectrum of students with significant cognitive, emotional, and physical and sensory disabilities will all be part of the central, core culture of the school.

Of course, there's not going to be an instant transformation, but I do think that disabled and nondisabled students will be used to one another, and used to working together in ways that faculty have never experienced. The faculty are more likely to remember a time when disabled students and nondisabled students went to different schools, or at least different classes, took different school buses, and were usually isolated from one another in school and play. Not many will have been in colleges and universities, as the entering freshmen class of 1996 was, where more than 10 percent of the students reported having disabilities (This year's freshmen 1997).

The students' college curriculum will also be out of step with their experience of a range of phenomena related to being disabled in late-twentieth-century America or of witnessing disability in these circumstances. Most of the students will not notice. Their high school classes will probably not have made mention of disability in any overt way. Disability is unlikely to have been employed as a perspective in their literature, current events, or biology classes. The dramatic changes in public education over the past twenty years would not have been interpreted for them. Although I hope that some mechanisms are put into place to teach young disabled people this history, to learn in substantive ways about their newly won rights, and to help them see the relationship between the personal and the political nature of the experience of disability, it is likely that that will not be consistently provided. Therefore, although both the disabled and nondisabled students coming up are likely to be more experienced, they will need the opportunity to interpret that experience within and throughout the curriculum. Otherwise, they will not understand the historical specificity of this moment, its meaning and significance, nor how to create meaningful change.

The arguments throughout this book in favor of integrating disability studies into the curriculum are not presented solely because more disabled students are entering college, or because disabled and nondisabled people will be interacting with one another in schools and in the community in ways that they never have before. The need to understand disability, and the construction of disability, clearly predates the present moment and extends beyond the boundaries of educational institutions. Moreover, as I've argued, there are epistemological reasons to debunk the primacy of medical interpretations of disability, to interpret metaphors of disability in order to bring more accurate readings to a text, to challenge the normal/abnormal dichotomies and all their manifestations, and to create theories or conduct research that is more representative, valid, and universal. Yet it would be a mistake to ignore the shifting culture of the schools and the changing student body in considering how curriculum is shaped.

In this chapter, rather than look inside the academic world, I turn the camera outward, toward the world that students inhabit when they leave college. Let's consider what they face and examine the reasons that a more substantive curriculum in disability studies is crucial for preparing disabled and nondisabled students for work and citizenship, including the specific preparation of disabled students to assume leadership roles in their communities, organizations, and workplaces. All of these students will meet with an array of issues that would benefit from, or are absolutely dependent on, a close disability analysis. As they leave school, or even in the course of their education, they will confront critical incidents—some taking up a few minutes, some complex and long-lasting—that will require experience in thinking about disability in a number of different domains, critical reasoning skills, and, often, a conscious well-considered sense of their own feelings about disability and disabled people. Both disabled and nondisabled students will encounter such incidents, and they will encounter them whether or not their work or community life directly involves disabled people or disability issues.

What follows are a few examples of some of these issues embedded in vignettes or case histories of persons in a job situation, or in family or community life. Imagine yourself in each situation and consider how well prepared you are to play out your role.

AN ASSISTANT CURATOR

You work at an art museum and are in charge of developing the written materials that accompany exhibitions. An installation of paintings by Goya is planned, and in preparation for that event you conduct research on the artist, his patronage, his subjects, and the historical period in which he worked. It occurs to you as you write the text for the audio guide, the pamphlet on the exhibit, and the commentary to be posted beside each painting that there are a number of disability themes and issues that could be explicated in these materials. You wonder if, and how, you might discuss the function of people of short stature in Goya's paintings and their function in the court of Charles IV. Should you point out the depictions of fictional monsters and the real people with anomalous bodies portrayed as monstrous? More important, should you comment on the tendency of Goya, and of viewers, to blur the distinctions between people and supernatural creatures? In other words, is it a good idea to provide an explicit disability studies reading of Goya's paintings?

You examine your old college textbook and wonder how to counter the received wisdom that the "follies and brutalities" Goya witnessed and his "increased infirmities, including deafness, combined to depress his outlook and led to his late 'dark style'" (Gardner 1970, 639). How can you, in the context of the overall mission of the exhibition, challenge the kinds of beliefs that you yourself have held, and surely other visitors to the exhibit may hold as well? Many who view the paintings will have taken the standard introductory art history course in college and read that "Goya presents with a straight face a menagerie of human grotesques who, critics have long been convinced, must not have had the intelligence to realize that the artist was caricaturing them" (637). Yet, you recognize that many visitors will be offended by that perspective, including people who have physical characteristics similar to those portrayed in Goya's paintings. They may well understand that they are being objectified and mocked in his paintings and are hoping that the accompanying materials will interpret Goya's motivation and discuss the consequence of those representations.

Now, rather than imagining that you are this curator, put yourself in the shoes of a college professor teaching future curators who will go on to write such materials. You might be a literature professor, or an art historian, biologist, ethicist, or sociologist. What is your responsibility to help students challenge ideas such as those found in Gardner's text, or to provide perspectives and information when even those covert messages are absent? If you are a psychology professor, is it logical to say that it is not your job, that the art history classes will provide the analysis of representations of disability? Instead, consider what you might say about reinforcement theory and stereotypes that might help a future curator and other students to understand how paintings or other representations may reinforce distorted views of disabled people. If you are a historian, what might you say about the function of marginal figures in the court of various kings and noblemen, and the particular role of people with anomalous bodies? You might turn to David Gerber's (1996) essay on the careers of people exhibited in freak shows to contextualize your discussion of the use of dwarfs as jesters in European courts from 1600 to 1800. If you teach art history, you might discuss the cultural history of the museum, and focus on the Musée Universel des Sourds-Muets, part of the Institute for the Deaf in France, and the Museum of Pathological Anatomy in London, which were representative of a "new direction in museology, towards the recording of the Other" (Mirzoeff 1995, 199). Such museums were indicative of a trend in the late nineteenth century that did not bring about greater exposure of disabled people's perspectives but, instead, resulted in the valorization of medical practice. In the case of the French museum, "[R]ather than promote the achievement of deaf artists, the museum sought to commemorate the modern triumph over deafness" (198).

If you, the assistant curator had taken such a class, you might well ask: In preparing this exhibition, what is my obligation to consider the moral, aesthetic, intellectual, psychological, and social questions that the paintings raise? What can any professor do to ensure that a future curator will, at least, consider writing about this element of a painter's work and possess the knowledge and perspectives needed to follow through on the project if she or he chooses to?

A PERSONNEL DIRECTOR

You are the new personnel director for a midsized company. Because of a number of factors, including an outreach effort that your predecessor organized a couple of years ago, the firm has hired several people with different disabilities. You have learned that a group of them have been meeting over the past six months. They appear to be well organized and call themselves the Disability Action Group (DAG). They have requested an appointment with you, and you anticipate that they want to discuss some remaining access issues, of which you are aware. When you meet, you find that their agenda is quite different. To your surprise, they present a five-page memo concerning the in-house hostile atmosphere and the failure of some managers to provide reasonable accommodations. The memo includes the following:

- Jokes that had been circulating on interoffice e-mail include a few whose targets were people of short stature and people with mental retardation. A member of DAG had sent an e-mail message to all employees that the jokes were offensive and should stop, but they continued to circulate for several days.

- A ramp had recently been installed to make a formerly inaccessible building accessible to employees who use wheelchairs. Before that, two disabled employees scheduled to move to the building had submitted a memo to the design team with suggestions on the type of ramp needed, its ideal location, and some safety measures to consider, and had asked that a member of DAG be included in meetings to design the ramp. Despite the initiative, the team had not included a member and had ignored most of their suggestions. The ramp exited the building in a deserted area of the parking lot, next to the door where garbage is removed. When the DAG coordinator confronted the design team and the manager in charge of safety issues with the facts that the garbage smells, that rats had been spotted in the area, and that the ramp imposed isolation, she was told that there was no other way to have installed the ramp, it was built to code, and new lights would make the ramp and lot safe.
- Further, the parking spaces designated for people with disabilities had often been used by other employees. DAG took up the matter with the Security Office, which began ticketing illegally parked cars. A week later, one of the signs with the wheelchair symbol had been defaced.
- The company had held the Christmas party in a restaurant not wheelchair accessible, and whose bathrooms are not accessible. A DAG member brought this to the attention the party planner and was told that somebody would carry him up the stairs; things were going to be fine; the location couldn't be changed because of company custom; and arrangements had already been made.
- An employee who is blind had asked for a different work station because of noise that at times drowns out her talking computer. The supervisor responded that he had already made enough adjustments for her; there was no other place available; and she should try to ignore the noise.

As you read the DAG memo, you recall that on another occasion a similar complaint had been made against the same supervisor. The charge had been dropped, but the supervisor had been warned by the Personnel Department that the company is legally and ethically bound to comply with such requests and they are to be taken seriously.

- An employee who uses a wheelchair reported that a man well known and respected in the company, has been behaving in ways that she identifies as both disability and sexual harassment. When she is going down the hall he begins pushing her wheelchair without asking permission. Her statements that she prefers to push her own chair are countered by remarks such as "Don't worry. I'm glad to help you out," "Give your arms a rest; you must get tired," "I like doing it; I push all the handicapped ladies' wheelchairs at church." On a number of occasions, he has jumped in front of her and opened the door to the Women's Room in such a way that he entered the room, obviously uninvited. He has sat next to her in the cafeteria a few times, insisting on talking about her disability and asking personal questions. She has tried consistently to tell him that his presence and attentions are not welcome, but he has not been deterred.

The company is proud of its responsible social practices and has been praised by the union and consumer groups. Your predecessor had also worked to have disabled people included as a protected group in the company's affirmative action policy. You must now figure out what the company's legal and ethical obligations are, what the impact of adverse publicity might be for the company if DAG "goes public" with its complaints, and what management issues might ensue if these well-informed and disgruntled employees speak out. It will be your job to handle DAG, to communicate to the company executives the nature of the complaints, and to finesse the interpersonal tensions that may arise from the airing of these issues.

After confirming the complaints' legitimacy you take the file home and spend a good part of the weekend mulling matters over. It is difficult to analyze the elements of the situation and to weigh the complaints. You alternate, at one time seeing a pattern of behaviors that constitute a hostile environment—which requires a systemic response—and at another time seeing isolated incidents that are neither as virulent nor as pervasive as alleged.

The complaints raise a number of questions. Is disability harassment equivalent to sexual harassment, in either nature of coercion or in consequences for the individual being harassed? How is unwanted physical contact with the woman's wheelchair similar to or different from the kinds of unwanted bodily contact that would be considered sexual harassment? Is entering the Women's Room, seemingly to "help" with the door, a sexually menacing behavior? Is an inaccessible restaurant comparable to a club that discriminates against African Americans or doesn't allow women to become members? What type of scale can be used to weigh these differences? If someone who uses a wheelchair is willing to be carried into the restaurant and is then given a table, can the restaurant be deemed to be discriminating? Is the *real* issue not whether the restaurant itself is accessible but what it means symbolically, ethically, and legally for the company to persist in using it? Should the employees most affected by a ramp have the right to a say in its placement and design? Although OSHA codes and ADA codes were adhered to, the codes don't cover every contingency.

Consider the preparation the actors in this drama need in order to engage in resolving this conflict. Who are the players? You, the personnel director, have an undergraduate degree in some liberal arts field and a master's degree in business or human services. Where in your academic career would you have obtained the tools to handle this situation? A graduate course or, more likely, a workshop on the ADA and employment issues would be inadequate to ground you in the complex issues presented here. Further, such courses and workshops rarely link disability issues to sexist and racist issues that arise in the workplace. Would a similarly conceived workshop on gender issues be sufficient to understand gender equity issues in the workplace and sexual harassment? What about the employees? Where would they have gained the knowledge to analyze the inequities, to recognize one another as members of a constituency group, and to coalesce around these issues? What of the other employees implicated in the charges—where would their disability training have come from? Where would the unaccommodating supervisor, the "helpful" employee, or the autonomous design team have had the opportunity to challenge their own beliefs or take on new ideas about disability?

Also consider how understanding and resolving each of these dilemmas can have an impact on other management and personnel concerns. One can read each complaint in terms of a particular disability issue, as well as in terms of its relationship to accepted codes of behavior, power differentials among employees and their impact on individual rights, and autocratic decisions and their impact on members of a group. A well-prepared personnel director might be able to contextualize these complaints and discuss them in terms of the broader problems that all companies face but not lose sight of the specific disability issues raised.

AN ARCHITECT

You are an architect in a midsize firm, in a midsize city, working on a midsize job. You are new in the firm, and this is your first solo project: a library; a small center, with an auditorium for cultural events and community meetings; and a playground. The center will be in a neglected downtown area, and the city has requested a building that will draw some attention to the area.

When you joined the firm, you discussed with your employers your commitment to innovative projects, particularly those that are models of integration and accommodation for people with disabilities. For the present project, you want to include a number of features that will go beyond the requirements of the ADA, in that they will integrate access into the overall concept of the building rather than being add-ons. Although the features could be replaced with standard "handicap"-access materials without compromising the overall design, you believe that a more innovative approach could have significant symbolic, functional, and aesthetic impact, and it will be your job to convince the city to back the plan.

As you anticipate creating the desired environment, you are stymied by your lack of experience with truly integrated and accommodating buildings. You are particularly interested in creating an entrance that declares your intention: rather than the standard ramp alongside the building—which separates people who use the ramp from people who use the steps—you envisage an entrance that weaves together steps and slopes so all visitors can enter and leave the building together and interact with one another as they do so. A second innovation you are considering takes some of the features required by the ADA, such as the signs in Braille in the elevators and on office doors, and embeds them in the surface texture of the walls as part of a visual and tactile design motif. You have already consulted with two people who are blind and who have expertise in signage; they are enthusiastic. You also want railings along hall walls for people who need assistance in walking. Again, rather than the standard-issue, utilitarian ADA-approved railings, you're considering a combination of materials to produce functional equivalent railings that look and feel like decorative molding.

You are working on the playground design, in consultation with teachers from an inclusive elementary school. It will have features that promote social interaction and cognitive development. For instance, the teachers suggested play spaces that encourage children to face one another, so children with hearing impairments can watch the hearing children's lips and follow other visual cues, or where two children who use sign language can talk with each other. You want to come up with spaces for children who use wheelchairs to transfer to platforms joined by shoots and slides. You are thinking about a mapping system that will enable children who are blind to find the play areas. As with the building, you want to make the map interesting to users; something the sighted and blind children can use together.

The theater would incorporate wheelchair seating in every section, so wheelchair users are not isolated in back rows. It would also include a technical studio where subtitles for films and captions for live performance could be devised, as well as audio descriptions.

Your dilemma: the city's allocation provides for access and accommodation based on a model that complies with the ADA, not for the features you are proposing. Further, the funds for the library cover access and accommodation only for patrons, not staff and performers. You had reflexively gone along with that thinking in giving your assent when you should have kept your mind open to all concerned.

Your presentation includes a rationale for your design that you hope will appeal to the civic leaders and others in attendance. Will the rationale "speak" to them? For instance, you describe how the integration of the Brailled information in a stuccoed wall relief invites sighted people to look and touch, to investigate and think about Braille rather than ignore it as something not for them. In much the same way that Andy Warhol's Campbell's soup cans or Christo's wrapping the Reichstag encourages us to think about those elements in a different way, everyday elements of life can be made more available and interesting to sighted people as well as to blind people. Even putting a sign in Braille and in print on the wall that says "Please touch" alters the environment, and suggests to sighted people that touch is an important means to access beauty, information, and ideas. These combined tactile features provide a shared experience in the same way that the step/slope combined entranceway invites ramp and stair users to travel together, and the playground spaces encourage disabled and nondisabled children to play together.

As a further example to explain your motivation, you point out how American Sign Language, long considered by the general public simply as a pragmatic solution to the "problem" of deafness, has been incorporated into staged performances as an aesthetic and communicative element. This has helped people see it as interesting and expressive. You are suggesting that a rethinking of ramps may be similarly conducive to an enlarged perspective on the active participation of disabled people. Further, you are suggesting that not much creative energy has been invested in ramps not because they are not as interesting as steps but because they are associated with disability. In saying that, you allude to the transformation in thinking about women's work and women's creative endeavors both of which have been considered of lesser merit because of their association with a devalued group.

I would like to think that architects with your commitment and expertise are graduating from universities after having been exposed to the philosophical underpinnings of such environments, and having acquired the desired technical expertise to design them. Although some degree holders may fall into that category, I don't believe that schools of architecture are consciously reshaping their curricula to prepare architects to meet these challenges.

Courses in disability studies could find a natural home in schools of architecture. For instance, a course could examine the history of spaces tailored for people with disabilities—from institutions to sheltered workshops, to the placement of special education classrooms in schools—and consider the aesthetic and ideological statements these spaces make. Another course might consider the architecture of containment and confinement, and look at institutions of all stripes, how they comment on their inhabitants and how they comment on the relationship between the inhabitants and those outside. A course in marginalized groups and marginalized spaces, cross-listed in departments of architecture, geography, urban planning, and sociology, could examine the parallels between the social status of women, of disabled people, and of members of the economic underclass, and the spaces designed for them. Texts such as Leslie Kanes Weisman's (1992) *Discrimination by Design: A Feminist Critique of the Man-Made Environment* that have been used to bring a gendered reading to architecture could be included with readings on disability to investigate the properties of the "nondisabled-made environment." Weisman points out that "gender, race, class, occupation, and other factors like age and disability collectively create distinctly different spatial experiences for people, even within the same environmental setting" (40). Her comments about the imbalance in numbers of bathrooms and toilets for women and men can be discussed in terms of the unavailability of accessible toilets for people with mobility impairments. Courses that look at disability reflectively rather than reflexively can help students think in sophisticated ways about environments that invite the participation of all people.

A TRAVEL AGENT

This is a comparison of two travel agents. Let's use me as a possible customer. I travel quite a bit. I use a wheelchair and need to have advance, practical information on what awaits me in regard to accessibility. Let's say I'm going to Ireland. My cousin has recently been there and recommends an agent she found reliable and pleasant, and who knows of many interesting out-of-the-way places. I call, and the agent says to me, as agents have done in the past, "Oh dear, we can't help you. You need one of the specialized travel services for 'handicapped' people; they will know what to do for you." The agent might even throw in a gratuitous comment such as "Maybe you'd be more comfortable traveling in the United States; Ireland doesn't have all the modern buildings and such."

Another agent might say, "Tell me where you want to go. I'll be glad to arrange your trip, but if it turns out that I can't obtain all the information you need, you may want to find a more knowledgeable agent."

In either case, I might wind up using a specialized travel agency, and it might turn out to be a good solution because such agencies have access to information. I use these examples not to weigh the merits of the individual agents but to analyze the process by which my choice is made.

This may seem like a small moment, and it may appear that there are inconsequential differences between the scenarios. However, the tone and substance of the agents' responses are indicative of differing ideas about disability. Whereas the first agent focuses on the particularity of my needs, the second frames her response in terms of the adequacy of her expertise. The first agent's assumption is that my needs would be taken care of elsewhere; the second's, that all travel agents have some responsibility to learn about access issues.

Consider how this vignette could have used other types of service providers or professionals. For instance, can a store owner or a gynecologist refuse me service? The personnel may be pleasant, patronizing, or nasty when they refuse me. They may turn me away because they don't want to be bothered or because they are truly underprepared. But the outcome is that disabled people have fewer options, and many times are left with no options.

How do we, as a society, conceptualize those limited options? As inevitable consequences of disability? As the results of the refusal of public and private service providers to be fully responsible to the public? We are so used to the idea that disability is a medical condition that requires specialized services and skills that it is often hard to conceptualize a provider's refusal as discrimination. If someone who is blind or uses a wheelchair comes into a store, can the owner refuse service and tell the person to leave? If a disabled woman wants to become a patient of the only gynecologist in her vicinity who participates in her medical plan, can the gynecologist refuse to accept her on the basis of lack of expertise in working with disabled women? Is the gynecologist responsible for obtaining the knowledge she does not have? Are medical schools responsible for training physicians in these areas? Are medical insurance providers responsible for paying an out-of-plan expert? If the woman's disability does not have a specific impact on her gynecological or obstetric needs and hence requires no specific medical expertise, is the gynecologist's refusal more likely to be considered discriminatory? For instance, if she has a visual impairment or mental retardation, can the gynecologist assert that the extra time or patience required in working with her is the basis for the refusal?

Disabled people can't rely on the goodwill and liberal outlook of service providers to meet their needs. Legislation must ensure consistent provision of service and freedom from discrimination. Legislators are dependent on researchers and theorists to determine what constitutes discrimination, to recognize how and where it occurs, and to develop the extralegislative means to counteract it. For instance, in considering the behavior of the two travel agents, on what basis can we determine if the first agent's response is discriminatory? What factors come into play in considering this issue? The importance of travel, and if it is, important for whom? Are pleasure, leisure, and recreation less important than essential services such as food and medical care? In other words, is it acceptable for a travel agent to turn someone down but not for a gynecologist to do so? These are complex questions related to theories of entitlement, democracy, capitalism, and the obligation of private enterprise to serve the public—not to mention the ethical aspects related to what a society deems right or wrong behavior.

THE DIRECTOR OF AN INDEPENDENT LIVING CENTER

A disabled woman with an undergraduate degree in political science and some graduate courses in social work, you run an independent-living center in a midsized city that employs twenty-five people, some full-time and some half-time. In addition to providing direct services to disabled people in the area, the center has been involved in initiatives related to disability issues. You have been an outspoken, articulate, and informed spokesperson for your disability community.

One day the mayor's assistant informs you that you have been appointed to a panel of representatives of constituency groups at the National Conference of Mayors in Washington, D.C. The panel, expected to get much media attention, is to address intergroup relations, and overlapping and competing concerns of constituency groups.

As you consider the assignment, you realize that although you are knowledgeable about disability issues, you feel unprepared to place those issues in a larger context. Your experience has been largely applied and largely local. You have learned disability history through your work and a few books. Your one disability studies course in college was a survey course; none of your other social sciences or humanities courses helped you to place disability in the context of other civil rights issues, other identity issues, or other social and political issues. How can you begin to conceptualize and help others to think about the relationship of disability to race, class, and gender? How can you articulate issues of power and privilege and the status of nondisabled people? How can you demonstrate why disability representation is needed in groups that formulate policy? How can you get people to generalize what they know about race, gender, sexual-orientation, and class discrimination to the processes that exclude disabled people from civic life?

Switch roles and consider how you, as this woman's college professor, might have helped lay the groundwork for this moment. In which courses might it have been useful for her to "work through" ideas about disability? Certainly for the Washington panel's presentation, courses in political science and sociology whose syllabi incorporated disability perspectives into discussions of community, constituency groups, democracy, and the welfare state would be a good start. Yet, even though that might have provided some nuts and bolts, a more comprehensive approach and a deeper analysis are warranted. For instance, the center's director might have been helped by a course on feminist inquiry and social change in which the ways that research can both serve activist agendas and contribute to academic inquiry are discussed. There she may have been encouraged to write a paper on the application of research to disability issues and to bring out some relevant examples in class discussions. With the help of the teacher and students, she would have begun to think about the means available to address disability "problems." In a course in gay and lesbian studies, the professor might have discussed the parallels between the formation of identity of lesbian and gay young people and of disabled young people. In growing up, these youngsters often struggle to establish identity because those around them have little information on, and many times can be hostile toward, the cultural specifics of being gay or being disabled. Such an introduction might have helped her think about the overlapping needs of lesbian/gay and disabled groups. Any other course that discussed social construction and included disability among the constructed categories would certainly have helped her focus on social contingencies rather than the individual nature of disability, an asset when thinking about disabled people as a constituency group.

What if the presentation in Washington goes well and you decide to pursue a doctorate that would prepare you to think about and act on national disability issues full time? If you go to former professors for advice, how well prepared will they be to steer you toward a meaningful program? Do programs exist to apply to? I myself would suggest that you join the Society for Disability Studies and attend the annual conference to network with faculty teaching disability studies.[1] Although there are no doctoral programs that I believe would specifically prepare you in disability policy and activism, there are a number of institutions where you might pursue a degree in a related area, with a concentration of courses in disability studies.[2]

You may have been actively thinking about disability throughout your college career, but if the curriculum did not specifically address it, you may have come to believe at some level that disability is not relevant to the study of literature, sociology, or political science. It may have been difficult for you to raise questions about disability in classes because the faculty were unreceptive or because of your discomfort with other students' reactions. It is the faculty's responsibility to open up discussion on disability, even when students are already motivated to think about disability. Otherwise, it will remain invisible and increasingly problematic in its invisibility.

PROGRAM DIRECTOR

For a number of years you have been the director of a service organization providing day programs to people with physical disabilities and mental retardation. The organization, which has more than one hundred employees, is working well. Donations are up, programs such as the sheltered workshop, the social activities, and the educational programs have attracted national attention because they are seen as innovative by professional groups and are well-attended.

However, the *Disability Rag,* a disability rights quarterly, publishes a scathing piece on the organization and your directorship. The writer asserts that the programs do not prepare disabled people for outside employment and do not foster independent living. Further, that you and the staff, with very few exceptions, are nondisabled; exceptions hold low-level jobs, and they have no say in how the organization is run. Moreover, the Board of Directors has never had a member who was disabled.

The writer acknowledges that many of the people who attend

the programs have mental retardation and don't have the type of professional training that would prepare them for management jobs but contends that other disabled people in the community would qualify but have not been hired. Additionally, the organization could facilitate the participation of people with mental retardation in planning and decision making. The writer also criticizes the organization's fund-raising activities, such as last year's bike-a-thon, which you perceived as a huge success, for having excluded people who cannot ride bikes, and hence most program participants. Only two of the day-program participants were invited to the evening ceremony following the event. They were seated at the head table, but speakers, using only first names, told the audience how much each of them liked the day program. The participants were not given a chance to voice their opinions directly but later told the reporter simply but clearly about their discomfiture and were critical of the center and staff—comments that appeared in the article.

It is likely that you and the administrative staffers have degrees in rehabilitation or special education. You have devoted your lives to working with people with disabilities. Yet you find, when the article is discussed at the staff meeting, that your academic background and professional experience have in no way prepared you for the moral, political, and intellectual challenge the controversy presents. To compound your problem, the ombudsperson hired by you to represent participants' interests has read the article to a group and explained a number of the points to them. That group has asked to speak with you.

What might have prepared you and the staff for this moment? How might you have anticipated some of these criticisms, and what might have motivated you to change the practices long before the article appeared? Of course, agency personnel might not experience the article as a threat to conscience or practices. You all may be convinced that your intentions and behavior are exemplary and that the criticism is of a "political" nature and outside the realm of professional conduct. You may not heretofore have encountered any ideas that would challenge the benevolence and humanitarian concern that you believe guide your endeavors.

Academic programs designed to prepare students to work with disabled people have a particular responsibility to evaluate their own philosophy and their own practice with respect to the issues discussed in this vignette. For instance, college students may hear in their classes that inclusion in public education is a good thing but observe that general education and special education are separate departments in the institutions they are attending. Accordingly, they are not being prepared to work in inclusive classrooms. Some of their professors may give an occasional lecture on the importance of the ADA, and the history of discrimination and oppression of people with disabilities in this country, yet students may note that there is only one faculty member with a disability in their department, that only a few of their professors have joined a group to pressure the university to make the campus more accessible, or that a faculty member in special education refuses to provide extra time on an exam for a student who has a learning disability. These disjunctures between the overt and the covert curriculum may make it more difficult for students to integrate and act on personal and social change. Both disabled and nondisabled students may be influenced by this hidden curriculum, but the particular tragedy for disabled students is that they may internalize the message that disability leadership and equality are not that important, even, or most conspicuously, in departments of special education and rehabilitation.

Students might get a different message if they observed their department developing an explicit affirmative action policy and inclusion policy and then pressuring for university-wide adoption. If students observed a department providing disabled students with the support needed to become professionals and to assume leadership roles, they might learn more directly that it is important to perpetuate independence and leadership when they become directors of day programs. If professors conducted outreach efforts to attract disabled students and wrote grants for scholarships for disabled students, they would demonstrate to students that they value disabled people's success and participation. If the faculty refused to participate in planning conferences or research projects on disability unless disabled people are a significant portion of the team, students would learn that their teachers are willing to practice what they preach. If faculty lobbied for the participation of disabled people and of people with expertise in disability studies in college-wide curriculum projects, students might learn that disability studies is part of diversity and multicultural agendas. If departments of special education and rehabilitation offered regularly scheduled courses in disability studies, students would find an excellent site to challenge established beliefs and practices and to consider their own ideas about disability as a socially constructed category. If students saw special education and general education faculty working together on an inclusive teacher-education curriculum they might learn how to create inclusive classrooms and schools once they graduate.

You, as the program director described here, may not have realized when you hired the ombudsperson or, when you agreed to let the writer from the *Rag* visit your organization, that your decisions would precipitate this critical moment. Yet, you're sure to recognize that even if this blows over, other people could disrupt the smooth flow of events in the future. A new participant may transfer into the program from a different city. She may come from a group home with an assisted-employment program, where she worked in the community with occasional support from a job trainer who monitored her work weekly. She may have gotten used to the autonomy, freedom, and income, and may resent the newly imposed limitations. She may urge the other participants to attend an administrative meeting and speak up about problems in the center. It's also possible that an employee might oppose current practice, based on differing views about what constitutes disabled people's rights. These kinds of confrontations are the outcome of paternalistic systems that seek to "care for" disabled people rather than support integration and accommodation in the community. If service providers are perceived as arrogant or supercilious by disabled people, even if their intention is to be supportive and to facilitate growth, we need to reexamine both the structure of our institutions as well the academic preparation of people who staff them.

A PARENT

You are a parent of a nondisabled young woman away at college. She calls to tell you she's bringing home a young man whom she is dating; he's "terrific, nice, smart, funny, and accomplished and has cerebral palsy." She tells you he uses a wheelchair and asks if you can get a large board he can use as a ramp to get into the house. She says his speech is sometimes hard to understand, but she'll be there and she's gotten so used to it; she understands pretty much everything.

When you hang up the phone, a flood of feelings and memories rush in. You recall sitting around the kitchen table twenty years ago with your brother and your parents, as your brother patiently explained that he was gay, that that wasn't going to change, and that he hoped that they would love him, accept him, and accept his partner. You wonder whether you will be open to accepting your daughter's partner, as you once hoped your parents would accept your brother's. You also recall that when your daughter was in kindergarten, a family moved in next door who had a disabled child named Rosie. You fought along with them to get the local school to set up an inclusive classroom that she could join. Your daughter and Rosie became friends, rode the school bus together, and attended each other's high school graduation parties. These memories and the pleasure you recall taking in your principled positions in each of these events did not prepare you for your disquiet and dismay at the prospect of your daughter's dating someone you anticipate feeling sorry for and uneasy around.

You recognize that your feelings might change once you meet him, but you also fear that they may not and that you may have to face the repercussions of being honest or of being dishonest when you see your daughter. You find yourself thinking about the same kinds of concerns your parents voiced to you about your brother, about how the rest of the family would perceive him and about how he would be an outcast in society. You realized then that these fears were a projection of your parents' personal feelings onto others, and now you find yourself running from your own feelings by attributing your own anxieties to others. You know that you are concerned about your daughter's well-being, and what you fear are her emotional and physical burdens if she marries a man with disabilities. On a deeper level you are aware that you have difficulty accepting that any man, and now you realize this man in particular will be having sex with your daughter, and simultaneously you fear that if your daughter marries this man, she may not have children.

A question that needs to be considered here is whether any curriculum,[3] even one with a full complement of disability studies material, can alter personal feelings such as yours. If you, as the parent described here, have made efforts to reduce the ableist practices in society but draw a line when personal commitments are at stake, can we consider your reaction ableist and can curriculum change such reactions? It is a question that is asked about racist, sexist, and homophobic feelings. Are these personal feelings and behaviors amenable to change by academic means or best left to interventions aimed at individuals or at social structures? Also, are ableism, racism, sexism, and heterosexism parallel issues? If so, and curricular change is implemented to address them, would the curricula have similar form, albeit some differing content?

Of course, I can't say for certain whether you, as the parent, would or would not be aided by courses in disability studies. I suspect that such previous exposure might prepare you for this internal struggle, if only to the extent that you would have had practice thinking consciously and deliberately about disability. Obviously, much more than curricular change is needed to alter such deeply held beliefs. Therefore, those of us who are outside the experience need an education in disability as well. Anyone attempting to think about, write about, and analyze such a moment, whether in teaching philosophy, writing a movie script, reporting for a newspaper, or counseling a parent at the local family center, or anyone who can potentially shape this moment would benefit from exposure to disability studies.

What if you were the young man about to meet your girlfriend's parents? What might help you to prepare for this meeting? If you anticipate or encounter hostility, pity, disgust, mawkishness, or awkward oversolicitousness in these people whom you want to get to know, want to have like you, what would prepare you not to be defensive or to personalize the parents' response? Although, again, your self-confidence, self-awareness, and social abilities might seem to be psychological variables, I can think of a hundred ways that a course in disability history or a literature class analyzing representations of disability might make you more resilient to the parents' interpretation of you. Maybe you could have taken a general liberal arts film course with a professor who incorporated disability perspectives into its content. Perhaps the professor showed *Guess Who's Coming to Dinner?* and asked the students to write papers on various alternative versions of the film. Rather than Katherine Ross's bringing home a "Negro," she may have invited someone of a different social class, or a woman with whom she was in love, or someone with a disability. Would the parents' response have been different or the same?

What if, in addition to such courses, there had been a disabled students' center at the university, built on the concept of disability culture and run by disabled students? What if you had organized a leadership training workshop or an outward bound program, where disability pride and disability leadership skills were taught—might that not bolster your internal resilience? Would you be helped by forming friendships with other disabled people your age or older who could tell you how they had fared in social encounters? These are lessons that your family, if they are nondisabled, and your nondisabled friends may not have much experience with.

Colleges and universities have in the past refused to admit disabled women and men, something they are not now permitted to do, and they now must provide access and accommodation. Yet they incur no legal sanctions if they don't tell the truth about disability. That is up to them to decide. For each discipline or area of study there are specific truths to be told. And specific lies. A lie that literature tells can be heard in the metaphors that create analogies between disability and insentience, or evil, or ineptness. Psychology tells lies when it reifies through theory and measurement the concept of normal. Anthropology's lies are found in the construction of a culture's ideas about disability, based solely on nondisabled people's input. History tells lies when it eliminates the perspectives of disabled people, and other marginalized people, from the annals of history, or eliminates information on public figures' disabilities. Women's studies lies when it excludes disabled women's perspectives, and then proceeds to make global statements about women's feelings and experience. Education proffers the idea that disabled and nondisabled children are separate groups best taught in separate classrooms by teachers separately trained. The lies told by clinical psychology and counseling are similar: disabled people's needs and problems are sufficiently different from nondisabled people's that specialists, called rehabilitation psychologists/counselors, are needed to treat them. Sociology fabricates a center, and then creates the concept of deviance to reinforce the centrality of nondisabled people. Medicine tells lies when it reduces differences to deficits, deficiencies, or pathologies. These are among the more obvious problems.

Disability studies tells a different story. Its tenets need to be worked through every discipline and field to assess their validity and applicability to a range of intellectual, social, political, and moral questions that we as a society face. The "truths" of disability studies will be revealed as we see how compromised the answers are without this perspective.

NOTES

1. The Society for Disability Studies is a national organization of scholars and activists. For information on the organization, write to Society for Disability Studies, Department of Public Management, Suffolk University, 8 Ashburton Place, Boston, Massachusetts 02108. For information on the journal *Disability Studies Quarterly*, write to Center for Disability Studies, University of Hawaii at Manoa, 1776 University Avenue, UA 4–6, Honolulu, Hawaii 96822.

2. An article by Pfeiffer and Yoshida (1995), "Teaching Disability Studies in Canada and the USA," lists some of those institutions and the courses taught.

3. Many people do not go to college and will not have access to the academic curriculum I am promoting. My focus in the book has been on higher education curriculum, but I believe that elementary and secondary schools will benefit from these ideas as well. In some ways, elementary schools have been addressing disability more deliberately than higher education has done. Although there are problems with that presentation—see chapter 4—schools have still attempted, through puppets, stories, American Sign Language demonstrations, and discussions about new children who will be included in the classroom, to talk openly about disability.

8

EPILOGUE

SOCRATES: So it was as a result of this profound discovery about his art that Tisias wrote that if a brave pygmy is prosecuted for assaulting a cowardly giant and robbing him of his clothes neither of them should reveal the truth. The coward must declare that he was attacked by more than one man, whereas his opponent must maintain that no one else was present and fall back on the well-known line: "How could a little chap like me have set upon a colossus like him?" The other of course will not admit his own poor spirit, but will produce some further lie which may provide his adversary with a chance of tripping him. And in other cases too these are the sort of "scientific" rules that are enunciated. Isn't it so Phaedrus?   Plato, *Phaedrus*

Covenants of the type Socrates described depend on both parties' agreeing to conform to social expectations, and depend on those witnessing the pact to suspend critical judgment. Socrates understood that sometimes the truth is kept secret in order not to upset the social order. The order rests on a simplified and reassuring version of the world. If giants cannot be counted on to be strong, and pygmies to be vulnerable and weak, we have to entertain the possibility of greater complexity and contradiction in all manner of other ideas as well. Indeed, what is compelling for me about Plato's tale, is not the morality fable about the hidden strengths of the weaker members of society, it is the tendency toward order and simplicity of thought that humans exhibit.

The introduction of disability studies into academic discourse is more significant as problematizing agent than as parable for the forgotten and downtrodden. It is, of course, on one level the voice of the pygmy, mad as hell and not willing to play the victim anymore. But it is more significantly the voice of the crowd, mature enough to take on the complex and difficult job of reordering society.

Stephen Greenblatt (1994) notes that those who uphold the traditional literary canon want a "tame and orderly canon. The painful, messy struggles over rights and values, the political and sexual and ethical dilemmas that great art has taken upon itself to articulate and grapple with, have no place in their curriculum" (290). As currently rendered, the academic curriculum devoted to disability is neatly bound in the specialized applied fields or in pathologizing constructs found in a few isolated spots in the rest of the curriculum. Similarly, society at large has attempted to keep disabled people in segregated schools and classrooms, institutions, back rooms, attics, and sheltered workshops.

Hidden and disregarded for too long, we are demanding not only rights and equal opportunity but are demanding that the academy take on the nettlesome question of why we've been sequestered in the first place. For, in disregarding disability as subject matter, disabled people as subjects, and disabled people's subjectivity, academics have been complicit in that confinement. Yet each of these elements, worked through the curriculum, can serve not only to liberate people but to liberate thought. Disability studies introduces contradiction into the polarized categories of weak and strong, normal and abnormal, revered and reviled, dependent and independent, expendable and essential. It reveals these as false dichotomies, and reveals the epistemological underpinnings of the privileged position in each pair. Other fields have described the consequences of the splits between public and private, personal and political, mind and body, or biological and social. Disability studies demonstrates how such compartmentalization often serves some groups better than others but ultimately serves no one well.

REFERENCES

Alcoff, L., and Potter, E. 1993. Introduction: When feminisms intersect epistemology. In L. Alcoff and E. Potter, eds., *Feminist epistemologies*, 1–14. New York: Routledge.

Allen, A. 1996. Open secret: A German academic hides his past—in plain sight. *Lingua Franca* 6 (3): 28–41.

American Heritage Dictionary. 1992. 3d ed. Boston: Houghton Mifflin.

Angier, N. 1995. How biology affects behavior and vice versa. *New York Times*, May 30, C1, C5.

Apple, M. W., and Christian-Smith, L. K., eds. 1991. *The politics of the textbook*. New York: Routledge.

Arokiasamy, C. V. 1993. A theory for rehabilitation? *Rehabilitation Education* 7: 77–98.

Asch, A., and Fine, M. 1988. Introduction: Beyond pedestals. In M. Fine and A. Asch, eds., *Women with disabilities: Essays in psychology, culture, and politics*. Philadelphia: Temple University Press.

Asch, A., and Rousso, H. 1985. Therapists with disabilities: Theoretical and clinical issues. *Psychiatry* 48: 1–12.

Baker, H. A., Jr. 1993. Multiculturalism: The task of literary representation in the twenty-first century. *Profession* 93: 5.

Barton, L., Ballard, K., and Fulcher, G. 1992. *Disability and the necessity for a socio-political perspective*. Durham, N.H.: International Exchange of Experts and Information in Rehabilitation.

Bérubé, M. 1996. *Life as we know it: A father, a family, and an exceptional child*. New York: Pantheon Books.

Bérubé, M., and Nelson, C. 1995. *Higher education under fire: Politics, economics, and the crisis of the humanities*. New York: Routledge.

Biklen, D. 1988. The myth of clinical judgement. *Journal of Social Issues* 44 (1): 127–40.

———. 1992. *Schooling without labels: Parents, educators, and inclusive education*. Philadelphia: Temple University Press.

Birdsell, J. D. 1972. *Human evolution: An introduction to the new physical anthropology*. Chicago: Rand McNally.

Bogdan, R. 1988. *Freak show: Presenting human oddities for amusement and profit*. Chicago: University of Chicago Press.

———. 1996. The social construction of freaks. In R. G. Thomson, ed., *Freakery: Cultural spectacles of the extraordinary body*, 23–37. New York: New York University Press.

Bogdan, R., and Taylor, S. 1987. Toward a sociology of acceptance: The other side of the study of deviance. *Social Policy* 18 (2): 34–39.

Brown, J. B. 1989. Societal responses to mental disorders in prerevolutionary Russia. In W. O. McCagg and L. Siegelbaum, eds., *The disabled in the Soviet Union: Past and present, theory and practice*, 13–37. Pittsburgh: University of Pittsburgh Press.

Brown, S. E. 1994. *Investigating a culture of disability*. (Available from the

Institute on Disability Culture, 2260 Sunrise Point Road, Las Cruces, New Mexico 88011).

Butler, J. E., and Walters, J. C. 1991. Praxis and the prospect of curriculum transformation. In J. E. Butler and J. C. Walters, eds., *Transforming the curriculum: Ethnic studies and women's studies*, 325–30. Albany: State University of New York Press.

Canguilhem, G. 1991. *The normal and the pathological.* New York: Zone Books.

Casanave, S. 1991. A community of friends and classmates. *Equity and Choice* 41: 38–44.

Coleman, R. L., and Croake, J. W. 1987. Organ inferiority and measured overcompensation. *Individual Psychology* 43 (3): 364–69.

Davis, L. J. 1995. *Enforcing normalcy: Disability, deafness, and the body.* London: Verso.

Edric, R. 1990. *In the days of the American museum.* London: Jonathan Cape.

Eiesland, N. L. 1994. *The disabled god: Toward a liberatory theology of disability.* Nashville, Tenn.: Abingdon Press.

Epstein, J. 1995. *Altered conditions: Disease, medicine, and storytelling.* New York: Routledge.

Farley, J. E. 1982. *Majority-minority relations.* Englewood Cliffs, N.J.: Prentice-Hall.

Ferguson, P. M., Ferguson, D. L., and Taylor, S. J., eds. 1992. *Interpreting disability: A qualitative reader.* New York: Teachers College Press.

Fine, M., and Asch, A., eds. 1988. *Women with disabilities: Essays in psychology, culture and politics.* Philadelphia: Temple University Press.

Frank, A. W. 1995. *The wounded storyteller: Body, illness and ethics.* Chicago: University of Chicago Press.

Fraser, N., and Gordon, L. 1994. A genealogy of dependency: Tracing a keyword of the U.S. welfare state. *Signs: Journal of Women in Culture and Society* 19 (2): 309–36.

Freilich, M., Raybeck, D., and Savishinsky, J. 1991. *Deviance: Anthropological perspectives.* New York: Bergin and Garvey.

Friedman, J. B. 1981. *The monstrous races in medieval art and thought.* Cambridge: Harvard University Press.

Funiciello, T. 1993. *Tyranny of kindness: Dismantling the welfare system to end poverty in America.* New York: Atlantic Monthly Press.

Gardner, H. 1970. *Art through the ages.* 5th ed. New York: Harcourt, Brace and World.

Gates, H. L., Jr. 1993. Beyond the culture wars: Identities in dialogue. *Profession* 93: 6–11.

———. 1996. White like me. *New Yorker* 72 (16): 66–81.

Gerber, D. A. 1996. The "careers" of people in freak shows: The problem of volition and valorization. In R. G. Thomson, ed., *Freakery: Cultural spectacles of the extraordinary body,* 38–54. New York: New York University Press.

Gill, C. J. 1994. Questioning continuum. In B. Shaw, ed., *The ragged edge: The disability experience from the pages of the first fifteen years of "The Disability Rag,"* 42–49. Louisville, Ky.: Advocado Press.

Gilman, S. L. 1985. *Difference and pathology: Stereotypes of sexuality, race, and madness.* New York: Cornell University Press.

———. 1988. *Disease and representation: Images of illness from madness to AIDS.* New York: Cornell University Press.

Gorelick, S. 1996. *Contradictions of feminist methodology.* In H. Gottfried, ed., *Feminism and social change: Bridging theory and practice.* Urbana: University of Illinois Press.

Gould, S. J. 1981. *The mismeasure of man.* New York: Norton.

———. 1988. Honorable men and women. *Natural History* 18: 16–20.

Graham, P. W., and Oehlschlaeger, F. H. 1992. *Articulating the Elephant Man: Joseph Merrick and his interpreters.* Baltimore: Johns Hopkins University Press.

Greenblatt, S. 1994. The politics of culture. In D. H. Richter, ed., *Falling into theory: Conflicting views on reading literature,* 289–93. Boston: Bedford Books of St. Martin's Press.

Groce, N. 1985. *Everyone here spoke sign language: Hereditary deafness on Martha's Vineyard.* Cambridge: Harvard University Press.

———. 1992. *The U.S. role in international disability activities: A history and look towards the future.* Oakland, Calif.: World Institute on Disability.

Groce, N., and Scheer, J. 1990. Introduction. *Social Science and Medicine* 30 (8): v–vi.

Grover, J. Z. 1987. AIDS: Keywords. In Douglas Crimp, ed., *AIDS: Cultural analysis*, 17–30. Cambridge: MIT Press.

Guillaumin, C., ed. 1995. *Racism, sexism, power, and ideology*. London: Routledge.

Hahn, H. 1987. Disability and capitalism: Advertising the acceptably employable image. *Policy Studies Journal* 15 (3): 551–70.

———. 1988. Can disability be beautiful? *Social Policy* 18 (winter): 26–31.

———. 1989. Disability and the reproduction of bodily images: The dynamics of human appearances. In J. Wolch and M. Dear, eds., *The power of geography: How territory shapes social life*, 370–88. Boston: Unwin Hyman.

Hanks, J. R., and Hanks, L. M., Jr. 1948. The physically handicapped in certain non-Occidental societies. *Journal of Social Issues* 13: 11–20.

Haraway, D. 1989. *Primate visions: Gender, race, and nature in the world of modern science*. New York: Routledge.

Harris, A., and Wideman, D. 1988. The construction of gender and disability in early attachment. In M. Fine and A. Asch, eds., *Women with disabilities: Essays in psychology, culture, and politics*. Philadelphia: Temple University Press.

Hartman, J. E., and Messer-Davidow, E., eds. 1991. *(En)gendering knowledge: Feminists in academe*. Knoxville: University of Tennessee Press.

Hentoff, N. 1997a. Death in the Netherlands. *Village Voice*, February 18, 20.

———. 1997b. Would your doctor kill? *Village Voice*, February 25, 22.

Herndl, D. 1993. *Invalid women: Figuring feminine illness in American fiction and culture, 1840–1940*. Chapel Hill: University of North Carolina Press.

Hevey, D. 1992. *The creatures time forgot: Photography and disability imagery*. London: Routledge.

Hirsch, K. 1995. Culture and disability: The role of oral history. *Journal of the Oral History Association* 22 (1): 1–27.

REFERENCES

Hockenberry, J. 1995. *Moving violations: War zones, wheelchairs, and declarations of independence*. New York: Hyperion.

Hubbard, R. 1990. *The politics of women's biology*. New Brunswick: Rutgers University Press.

Huet, M. H. 1993. *Monstrous imagination*. Cambridge: Harvard University Press.

Ingstad, B., and Whyte, S. R., eds. 1995. *Disability and culture*. Berkeley: University of California Press.

Kailes, J. I. 1995. *Language is more than a trivial concern!* (Available from June Isaacson Kailes, Disability Policy Consultant, 6201 Ocean Front Walk, Suite 2, Playa del Rey, California 90293–7556)

Keller, E. F. 1985. *Reflections on gender and science*. New Haven: Yale University Press.

Kent, D. 1988. In search of a heroine: Images of women with disabilities in fiction and drama. In M. Fine and A. Asch, eds., *Women with disabilities: Essays in psychology, culture, and politics*, 90–110. Philadelphia: Temple University Press.

Kliebard, H. M. 1992. *Forging the American curriculum: Essays in curriculum history and theory*. New York: Routledge.

Kohl, H. 1994. On forcing the integration of black colleges. *Journal of Blacks in Higher Education* (autumn): 92–93.

Kriegel, L. 1969. Uncle Tom and Tiny Tim: Some reflections on the cripple as negro. *American Scholar* 412–30.

———. 1982. The wolf in the pit in the zoo. *Social Policy* (fall): 16–23.

Kristof, N. D. 1996. Outcast status worsens pain of Japan's disabled. *New York Times*, April 7, 3.

Liazos, A. 1972. The poverty of the sociology of deviance: Nuts, sluts, and preverts. *Social Problems* 20 (1): 103–20.

Lilly, M. 1989. Teacher preparation. In D. Lipsky and A. Gartner, eds., *Beyond separate education*, 143–57. Baltimore, Md.: Brookes.

Linton, S. 1990. Sexual satisfaction in men following spinal cord injury as a function of locus of control. *Rehabilitation Psychology* 35: 19–27.

———. 1994. Reshaping disability in teacher education and beyond. *Teaching Education* 9: 9–20.

———. 1996. The disability studies project: Broadening the parameters of diversity. In E. Makas and L. Schlesinger, eds., *End results and starting points: Expanding the field of disability studies*, 323–27. Portland, Maine: Society for Disability Studies and Edmund S. Muskie Institute of Public Affairs.

Linton, S., Mello, S., and O'Neill, J. 1994. Locating disability in diversity. In E. Makas, and L. Schlesinger, eds., *Insights and outlooks: Current trends in disability studies*, 229–33. Portland, Maine: Society for Disability Studies and Edmund S. Muskie Institute of Public Affairs.

———. 1995. Disability studies: Expanding the parameters of diversity. *Radical Teacher* 47: 4–10.

Linton, S., and Rousso, H. 1988. Sexuality counseling with people who have disabilities. In E. Rosen and S. Weinstein, eds., *Sexuality counseling*, 114–34. Pacific Grove, Calif.: Brooks/Cole.

Longmore, P. K. 1985a. A note on language and the social identity of disabled people. *American Behavioral Scientist* 28 (3): 419–23.

———. 1985b. The life of Randolph Bourne and the need for a history of disabled people. *Reviews in American History* 586 (December): 581–87.

———. 1987. Uncovering the hidden history of people with disabilities. *Reviews in American History* 15 (3) (September): 355–64.

Mairs, N. 1996. On being fair to strangers. Review of *Life as we know it: A father, a family, and an exceptional child*, by Michael Bérubé. *Nation*, 263 (13): 30.

Mallory, B. L. 1993. Changing beliefs about disability in developing countries: Historical factors and sociocultural variables. In D. Woods, ed., *Traditional changing views of disability in developing societies*. Durham: University of New Hampshire and World Rehabilitation Fund.

McCagg, W. O. 1989. The origins of defectology. In W. O. McCagg and L. Siegelbaum, eds., *The disabled in the Soviet Union: Past and present, theory and practice*, 39–62. Pittsburgh: University of Pittsburgh Press.

McCagg, W. O., and Siegelbaum, L. 1989. Introduction. *The disabled in the Soviet Union: Past and present, theory and practice*, 3–10. Pittsburgh: University of Pittsburgh Press.

McLaren, P. 1994. *Life in schools: An introduction to critical pedagogy in the foundations of education*. White Plains, N.Y.: Longman.

Messer-Davidow, E. 1991. Academic knowledge and social change. In

J. Hartman and E. Messer-Davidow, eds., *(En)gendering knowledge: Feminists in academe*, 281–309. Knoxville: University of Tennessee Press.

Minnich, E. K. 1990. *Transforming knowledge.* Philadelphia: Temple University Press.

Minow, M. 1990. *Making all the difference: Inclusion, exclusion and American law.* Ithaca: Cornell University Press.

Mirzoeff, N. 1995. *Silent poetry: Deafness, sign, and visual culture in modern France.* Princeton: Princeton University Press.

Morris, D. B. 1991. *The culture of pain.* Berkeley: University of California Press.

Mudrick, N. 1983. Disabled women. *Society* 20 (3): 52–55.

Mydral, G. 1944. *An American dilemma: The negro problem and modern democracy.* With the assistance of Richard Sterner and Arnold Rose. 2 vols. New York: Harper and Brothers.

National Center on Educational Restructuring and Inclusion. 1995. *National study on inclusive education.* New York: City University of New York, The Graduate School and University Center.

Nichols, R. W. 1993. An examination of some traditional African attitudes towards disability. In D. Woods, ed., *Traditional changing views of disability in developing societies.* Durham: University of New Hampshire and World Rehabilitation Fund.

Nieto, S. 1992. *Affirming diversity: The sociopolitical context of multicultural education.* New York: Longman.

Norden, M. F. 1994. *The cinema of isolation: A history of physical disability in the movies.* New Brunswick: Rutgers University Press.

Oakes, J. 1985. *Keeping track: How schools structure inequality.* New Haven: Yale University Press.

Oliver, M. 1992. Changing the social relations of research production. *Disability, handicap, and society* 7 (2): 101–14.

Orsi, R. A. 1994. "Mildred, is it fun to be a cripple?": The culture of suffering in mid-twentieth-century American Catholicism. *South Atlantic Quarterly* 93 (3): 547–90.

Padden, C., and Humphries, T. 1988. *Deaf in America: Voices from a culture.* Cambridge: Harvard University Press.

194

Peterson, S. V. 1993. Disciplining practiced/practices: Gendered states and politics. In E. M. Davidow, D. R. Shumway, and D. J. Sylvan, eds., *Knowledges: Historical and critical studies in disciplinarity*, 243–67. Charlottesville: University of Virginia Press.

Pfeiffer, D. 1994. Eugenics and disability discrimination. *Disability and Society* 9 (4): 481–99.

Pfeiffer, D., and Yoshida, K. 1995. Teaching disability studies in Canada and the USA. *Disability and Society* 10 (4): 475–95.

Phillips, M. J. 1985. "Try harder": The experience of disability and the dilemma of normalization. *Social Science Journal* 22 (4): 45–57.

Plato. 1973. *Phaedrus and the seventh and eighth letters* Translated with introduction by Walter Hamilton. Middlesex, Eng.: Penguin Books.

Polakow, V. 1993. *Lives on the edge: Single mothers and their children in the other America.* Chicago: University of Chicago Press.

Post, J. M., and Robins, R. S. 1990. The captive king and his captive court: The psychopolitical dynamics of the disabled leader and his inner circle. *Political Psychology* 11: 331–51.

Radford, J. P. 1994. Intellectual disability and the heritage of modernity. In M. H. Rioux and M. Bach, eds., *Disability is not measles: New research paradigms in disability*, 9–27. North York, Ontario: L'Institut Roeher Institute.

Reed, A., Jr. 1995. The scholarship of backlash. Review of *Turning back: The retreat from racial justice in American thought and policy*, by Stephen Steinberg. *Nation* (October 30): 506–10.

Rioux, M. H., and Bach, M., eds. 1994. *Disability is not measles: New research paradigms in disability.* North York, Ontario: L'Institut Roeher Institute.

Rosenburg, C. E., and Golden, J., eds. 1992. *Framing disease: Studies in cultural history.* New Brunswick: Rutgers University Press.

Ross, J. A. 1983. An anthropological view of the change in attitudes toward mental illness and physical handicaps. *History and Social Science Teacher* 135–40.

Rothman, D. J. 1980. *Conscience and convenience: The asylum and its alternatives in progressive America.* Boston: Little Brown.

Rousseau, G. S. 1978. Literature and science: The state of the field. *ISIS* 69: 583–91.

———. 1981. Literature and medicine: The state of the field. *ISIS* 72: 406–24.

Rubin, H. H. 1933. *Eugenics and sex harmony: The sexes, their relations and problems.* Boston: Paramount.

Russo, M. 1994. *The female grotesque: Risk, excess, and modernity.* New York: Routledge.

Sacks, O. 1988. The revolution of the deaf. *New York Review of Books* (June 2): 23–28.

Sagarin, E. 1971. *The other minorities: Nonethnic collectivities conceptualized as minority groups.* Waltham, Mass.: Xerox College Publishing.

Sampson, E. E. 1993. Identity politics: Challenges to psychology's understanding. *American Psychologist* 48 (12): 1219–30.

Scheer, J. 1994. Culture and disability: An anthropological point of view. In E. J. Trickett, R. J. Watts, and D. Birman, eds., *Human diversity: Perspectives on people in context,* 244–60. San Francisco: Jossey-Bass.

Scheer, J., and Groce, N. 1988. Impairment as a human constant: Cross-cultural and historical perspectives on variation. *Journal of Social Issues* 26: 23–37.

Scheer, J., and Luborsky, M. L. 1991. The cultural context of polio biographies. *Orthopedics* 14 (11): 1173–81.

Schuster, M. R., and Van Dyke, S. R., eds. 1985. *Women's place in the academy: Transforming the liberal arts curriculum.* Totowa, N.J.: Rowman and Allanheld.

Schwartz, D. B. 1992. *Crossing the river: Creating a conceptual revolution in community and disability.* Cambridge, Mass.: Brookline Books.

Sedgwick, E. K. 1990. *Epistemology of the closet.* Berkeley: University of California Press.

Sesser, S. 1994. Hidden death. *New Yorker* 64 (November 14): 62–90.

Shakespeare, T. 1996. Review of *An anthropologist on Mars,* by Oliver Sacks. *Disability and Society* 11 (1): 137–42.

Shapiro, J. P. 1993. *No pity: People with disabilities forging a new civil rights movement.* New York: Times Books.

Shumway, D. R., and Messer-Davidow, E. 1991. Disciplinarity: An introduction. *Poetics Today* 12 (2): 201–25.

Siegel, H. 1995. What price inclusion? *Teachers College Record* 97 (1): 6–31.

Silvers, A. 1995. Reconciling equality to difference: Caring (f)or justice for people with disabilities. *Hypatia* 10 (1): 30–55.

Skrtic, T. M. 1992. The special education paradox: Equity as the way to excellence. In T. Hehir and T. Latus, eds., *Special education at the century's end*, 203–72. Cambridge: Harvard Educational Review.

Sleeter, C. E., and Grant, C. A. 1991. Race, class, gender and disability in current textbooks. In M. W. Apple and L. K. Christian-Smith, eds., *The politics of the textbook*, 78–110. New York: Routledge.

Sontag, S. 1978. *Illness as metaphor.* New York: Farrar, Straus and Giroux.

———. 1990. *Illness as metaphor and AIDS and its metaphors.* New York: Anchor Books.

Stainback, S., and Stainback, W. 1985. *Integration of students with severe handicaps into regular schools.* Reston, Va.: Council for Exceptional Children.

Starr, P. 1982. *The Social transformation of American medicine: The rise of a sovereign profession and the making of a vast industry.* New York: Basic Books.

Stedman's Medical Dictionary. 1976. 23d ed. Baltimore: Williams and Wilkins.

Szasz, T. 1990. *Insanity: The idea and its consequences.* New York: John Wiley.

———. 1991. *Ideology and insanity: Essays on the psychiatric dehumanization of man.* New York: Syracuse University Press.

Tavris, C. 1991. The mismeasure of woman: Paradoxes and perspectives in the study of gender. In J. D. Goodchilds, ed., *Psychological perspectives on human diversity in America*, 87–137. Washington, D.C.: American Psychological Association.

———. 1992. *The mismeasure of woman.* New York. Simon & Schuster.

This year's freshmen: A statistical profile. 1997. *Chronicle of Higher Education* (January 17): A42.

Thomson, R. G. 1990. Speaking about the unspeakable: The representation of disability as stigma in Toni Morrison's novels. In J. Glasgow and A. Ingram, eds., *Courage and tools: The Florence Howe Award for Feminist Scholarship, 1974–1989*, 238–51. New York: Modern Language Association.

———. 1994. Redrawing the boundaries of feminist disability studies. *Feminist Studies* 20: 583–95.

———. 1997. *Extraordinary bodies: Figuring physical disability in American culture and literature.* New York: Columbia University Press.

———, ed. 1996. *Freakery: Cultural spectacles of the extraordinary body.* New York: New York University Press.

Thurston, A. F. 1996. In a Chinese orphanage. *Atlantic Monthly* 40 (April): 28–41.

Todd, A. D. 1984. Women and the disabled in contemporary society. *Social Policy* 44 (spring): 44–46.

Tremblay, M. 1996. Going back to civvy street: A historical account of the Everest and Jennings wheelchair for Canadian World War II veterans with spinal cord injury. *Disability and Society* 11 (2): 149–69.

Trent, J. W., Jr. 1994. *Inventing the feeble mind: A history of mental retardation in the United States.* Berkeley: University of California Press.

Trickett, E. J., Watts, R. J., and Birman, D. 1994. Toward an overarching framework for diversity. In E. J. Trickett, R. J. Watts, and D. Birman, eds., *Human diversity: Perspectives on people in context,* 7–80. San Francisco: Jossey-Bass.

Trinkhaus, E., and Shipman, P. 1993. *The Neanderthals: Changing the image of mankind.* New York: Knopf.

Tulloch, S., ed. 1993. *The Reader's Digest Oxford wordfinder.* Oxford, Eng.: Clarendon Press.

Ward, L., and Flynn, M. 1994. What matters most: Disability and empowerment. In M. H. Rioux and M. Bach, eds., *Disability is not measles: New research paradigms in disability,* 29–48. North York, Ontario: L'Institut Roeher Institute.

Watkins, W. H. 1994. Multicultural education: Toward an historical and political inquiry. *Educational Theory* 106 (winter): 99–117.

Waxman, B. F., and Gill, C. J. 1996. Sexuality and disability: Misstate of the arts? Review of *Physical medicine and rehabilitation state of the arts review: Sexuality and disability,* edited by Trilok N. Monga. *Journal of Sex Research* 33 (3): 267–70.

Wehman, P. 1993. *The ADA mandate for social change.* Baltimore: Paul H. Brookes.

Weiner, F. 1986. *No apologies: Making it with a disability.* New York: St. Martin's Press.

Weisman, L. K. 1992. *Discrimination by design: A feminist critique of the man-made environment.* Urbana: University of Illinois Press.

Wendell, S. 1989. Toward a feminist theory of disability. *Hypatia* 4: 104–26.

———. 1996. *The rejected body: Feminist philosophical reflections on disability.* New York: Routledge.

Whyte, S. R. 1995. Disability between discourse and experience. In B. Ingstad and S. R. Whyte, eds., *Disability and culture,* 267–91. Berkeley: University of California Press.

Wilford, J. N. 1994. Sexes equal on South Sea isle. *New York Times,* March 29, C1, C11.

Williams, J. 1993. Sedgwick unplugged: An interview with Eve Kosofsky Sedgwick. *Minnesota Review* 52–64.

Young, Iris Marion. 1990. *Justice and the politics of difference.* Princeton: Princeton University Press.

Zalewski, D. 1995. Unfriendly competion. *Lingua Franca* 5 (September/ October): 19–21.

Zborowski, M. 1960. *People in pain.* San Francisco: Jossey-Bass.

Zola, I. K. 1987. The portrayal of disability in the crime mystery genre. *Social Policy* 18 (2): 34–39.

INDEX

ABOUT THE AUTHOR

SIMI LINTON is Associate Professor in the Department of Educational Foundations and Counseling Programs at Hunter College–CUNY and teaches courses in the psychological foundations of education and in disability studies.

Her research interests are primarily in disability studies and in sexuality, and she was the founder and the first chairperson of the National Coalition on Sexuality and Disability. In 1995 she was a recipient of a Switzer Distinguished Fellowship from the United States Department of Education's National Institute on Disability and Rehabilitation Research. She is currently at work on a collection of essays on the disability experience entitled *Disability Stories.*

CPSIA information can be obtained
at www.ICGtesting.com
Printed in the USA
JSHW040244070722
27861JS00002B/303